30 YEARS OF THE FREEDOM CHARTER

RAYMOND SUTTNER ● JEREMY CRONIN

with contributions by:
● Mosiuoa 'Terror' Lekota ● Dorothy Nyembe ● Wilson Fanti ●
Edgar Ngoyi ● Steve Tshwete ● Popo Molefe ● Bishop Manas Buthelezi
Billy Nair ● Cheryl Carolus ● Rev Frank Chikane ●
Fr Smangaliso Mkatshwa ●

Ravan Press   Johannesburg

Published by Ravan Press (Pty) Ltd.,
P.O. Box 31134, Braamfontein 2017, South Africa

© Raymond Suttner and Jeremy Cronin

All rights reserved. No part of this publication may be reproduced, stored in a retrieval system, or transmitted in any form or by any means, electronic, mechanical, photocopying, recording, or otherwise, without the prior permission of the Copyright owner.

First impression 1986

ISBN 0 86975 299 5

Cover Art: Graphic Equaliser
Typesetting: Setbold and Planographic
Printed and bound: Interpak Natal
Layout: New Art

Produced by Raymond Suttner and Jeremy Cronin in conjunction with the History Resources Project.

To the men, women and children who have sacrificed their lives in the struggle to realise the Freedom Charter.

Contents

1. Foreword ix

A. THE CONGRESS OF THE PEOPLE CAMPAIGN 1

I. Introduction 3
2. Recovering the people's history 4
3. Reggie and Shirish 6

II. The volunteers 11
4. "An organiser of the people" 12
5. Document: "To all volunteers" 17
6. Document: "Listen young friend" 21

III. Collecting demands 25
7. "A two card carrying member" 26
8. Cradock, the cradle of the Charter 31
9. "The first question was the land" 35
10. The workers' demands 39
11. "I can do something in the organiser side" 44
12. "Straight away you're a comrade" 47
13. "He comes to his sober senses" 52
14. "People not having land of their own" 57
15. Document: "Call to the Congress of the People" 63

IV. Electing delegates — 69
16. The study class in Blouvlei — 70
17. Document: "Let us speak of freedom" — 74

V. Travelling to Kliptown — 79
18. Whistling the Internationale in Beaufort West — 80

VI. Kliptown, June 25 26th, 1955 — 85
19. The first day — 86
20. The second day — 98

VII. Reporting back — 105
21. "Conveying the message, house to house" — 106

VIII. Rumblings within — 111
22. "Congress has something up its sleeve!" — 112

IX. The Treason Trial — 117
23. "The Charter was in the front line now" — 118

X. The Charter lives on — 121
24. A goatskin tobacco pouch — 122

B. UNDERSTANDING THE CHARTER — 125

XI. What type of document is the Freedom Charter? — 127
25. The Freedom Charter, the People's Charter — 128

XII. To whom does South Africa belong? — 131
26. "South Africa belongs to all who live in it, black and white..." — 132

XIII. The Charter, the national question and culture — 135
27. One people, many cultures — 136
28. Mzwakhe: "Culture must be a weapon" — 138

XIV. The Freedom Charter and the working class — 141
29. In the workers' interests — 143

XV. The Freedom Charter and women — 149
30. Struggling shoulder to shoulder — 150
31. Carolus: "Things don't happen automatically" — 152
32. Kwadi: Women's demands are the people's demands — 158
33. Document: "The women's charter" — 161
34. Document: "The women's demands for the Freedom Charter" — 167

XVI. The land question — 173
35. The first demand in the rural areas was for land — 174

XVII. The Freedom Charter and the petit-bourgeoisie — 177
36. Our struggle is national — 178

XVIII. The Freedom Charter and education — 181
37. Opening the doors of learning — 182
38. Johnson: Four cuts for the Charter — 187

XIX. "There shall be peace and friendship" — 189
39. No peace under apartheid — 190

C. THE CHARTER TODAY — 193

XX. Lekota: In search of the Charter — 195

40. A personal account ... 196

XXI. Molefe: UDF and the Freedom Charter ... 205
41. Two documents — a single vision ... 206

XXII. Tshwete: A People's Charter ... 209
42. Understanding the Charter clause by clause ... 210

XXIII. The Freedom Charter and religion ... 221
43. Mkatshwa: The Freedom Charter — a theological critique ... 222
44. Xundu: "I was present when the Charter was adopted" ... 225
45. Nolan: The Freedom Charter and the Christian Churches ... 227
46. Kearney: "...and owned everything in common" ... 230
47. Tutu and Naude: Our common humanity ... 232
48. Chikane: "It depends on where you key in" ... 235
49. Buthelezi: "There is nothing unchristian about the Charter" ... 238
50. Langeveld: A challenge to the Church ... 240
51. Solomon: Islam and the Freedom Charter ... 244

XXIV. Organising with the Freedom Charter ... 247
52. The Freedom Charter as an organising tool ... 248

XXV. Footnotes ... 257
53. Footnotes ... 258

XXVI. The Freedom Charter ... 261
54. The Freedom Charter ... 262

1. Foreword

This book tries to recover a crucial aspect of South African history — the making of the Freedom Charter. The Freedom Charter has a unique authority because of the mode of its creation. Never before, or since, have the people of South Africa themselves put down their own vision of the type of society in which they would like to live.

In one sense the adoption of the Charter represented a continuation of earlier resistance. But in another sense, it marked the start of a new phase in the South African struggle. For the first time in the history of South African resistance, the people were actively involved in formulating their own vision of an alternative society. The majority of people would no longer seek to modify the existing order, to be assimilated into a society whose basis they fundamentally rejected. While the process by which the masses had come to this decision had been developing over decades, the Congress of the People represented the crucial historical moment: a completely new order, based on the will of the people, was put on the agenda.

This decision has considerable relevance today. From the moment of the adoption of the Charter, all political solutions 'from above' were ruled out. That is why, even if a 'fourth chamber' or any similar forum were today offered to Africans under the present constitution, it would still be rejected. From the time of the adoption of the Charter, the people have been unwilling to accept any 'solutions' that fall short of its demands and are not of their own creation.

For many years state repression made it difficult to obtain the Charter or to propagate it. Certainly it was hard to find out about the Congress of the People campaign. The suppression of popular history facilitates oppression. Oppressors know that people draw inspiration from the struggles and traditions of the past.

The recovery of the history of democratic struggle is therefore part of the process of freeing South Africa.

The Freedom Charter was created in a period of massive development of popular organisation — the 1950s. It is well-known that the extreme repression of the 1960s and most of the 1970s halted this process, and that many South Africans have in fact grown up ignorant of its existence.

It is no coincidence that the continued significance of the Freedom Charter is now reasserted — in the mid-1980s, a period when mass democratic struggle has again emerged.

There is another significant similarity between the period of 1955 and today. The Congress of the People campaign was initiated after the successful Defiance Campaign. The campaign to defy unjust laws represented a fundamental challenge to the apartheid regime. The Congress of the People campaign sought to take this crucial, though essentially negative campaign further. While continuing to reject racist laws, the campaign to create the Freedom Charter raised the positive vision of an alternative, apartheid-free South Africa.

In 1985 the oppressed and democratic people of South Africa have recently emerged from successful campaigns to boycott Black Local Authority and tricameral parliament elections. Thousands continue to boycott bantu education and the pass laws are rejected as unequivocally as ever. These and other institutions of racist rule can claim no popular legitimacy.

But, as in 1955, the people are taking this process further. They are again asserting the vision of a South Africa free from oppression and exploitation, the South Africa of the Freedom Charter.

In presenting this account of the creation of the Freedom Charter we have barely scratched the surface. There are many more people who know a great deal about the history of this period, from whom we have much to learn.

We need to talk to them, listen to them, and write down their story. We therefore view what we have done as part of a larger project which we hope others will undertake, to recover the people's history. We realise, however, that while many leading participants in the Congress of the People campaign remain imprisoned, exiled, banned, listed and unquotable, this history will remain incomplete.

This account of the Congress of the People campaign has been made possible by the assistance of very many people. Many older activists were kind enough to discuss their experiences at length and to introduce us to other participants. In some cases, interviews were conducted by trade unionists and activists from other democratic organisations. Our thanks to them all, as well as to those who allowed us to use material that they had gathered in the course of other research. There were many others who helped with typing, proofreading and photographs.

November, 1985

A.
THE CONGRESS OF THE PEOPLE CAMPAIGN

"Yo-yo-yo-yo,
my rusted
memory"

I. Introduction

2. Recovering the people's history

Our struggle is also a struggle of memory against forgetting

The apartheid regime has tried to wipe out all memory of the mass struggles of the 1950s. Leading political organisations of the time have been outlawed. Leaders and ordinary people have been jailed or been forced into exile; others were killed. Some have been banned or listed, their words, their memories becoming unquotable. Books, pamphlets, posters, badges, flags were seized in numerous police raids, or were censored into silence. Years of campaigning, mass struggles involving millions of people, all of these the system has tried to cast into permanent oblivion.

We, on our side, have comforting words, of course — *The people's power is irresistible! Our traditions can never die!* These are true enough.... Yes, in their way. But it is never simply guaranteed that the past, our past, this great store of lessons, will be remembered.

Our struggle is also a struggle of memory against forgetting.

Our search for those who remembered the Freedom Charter campaign took us, and many others who helped, all over South Africa In Worcester a student from Cape Town spoke to an old African man. He was barefoot, worked as a nightwatchman and lived all alone on the premises of a factory.

"Ja", said the old man, he remembers the Freedom Charter campaign, he remembers a meeting at Worcester addressed by "a tall thin one, a *rooikop* with glasses." We check the records, but we cannot work out who the particular 'red head' was. "He told us", recalls the nightwatchman, *"ons moet 'n Freedom Charter boek maak."*

How many others in our streets, townships, factories, on the buses, remember that huge campaign? We were able to speak to only a few of them. As we learned from them about that period, we also realised we were learning about the lives, the different backgrounds, the incredible experiences, hardships, and above all, bravery of ordinary South Africans.

Here we are in a small, tidy house in one of the African townships outside Cape Town. We are with an old comrade. He was politically active already, way back, in the 1940s. We have come, we say, to speak about the Kliptown Congress of the People in 1955. He looks uncomfortable. He shifts in his chair, wiping his brow.

"1955? The Congress of the People? You know comrades, since after 1963 when I spent six months in solitary confinement, my memory is not so good. But ask me some questions, perhaps that will help my memory. [Sadly shaking his head] Yo-yo-yo-yo, my rusted memory."

"You didn't of course get to Kliptown, comrade?"

"Oh yes! I was there."

"But wasn't the Western Cape delegation stopped at Beaufort West?"

"Not at all. Some of us got through in cars. [Silence...a long silence.] I was in a car with a senior comrade, Albert Matinya, from Stellenbosch in those days, and I think Ben Turok, and, let me see..."

The comrade slowly begins to tell us his story. Reaching back into that time, into that history that belongs to all of us, and which he carries there, in his head. It is the history the apartheid regime thought we had forgotten.

This is the story of the Freedom Charter, and of the Congress of the People campaign. It is told by many individuals, still living today in all parts of our country.

The struggle is also a struggle of memory against forgetting.

3. Reggie and Shirish

All over South Africa today there are those who remember the Freedom Charter campaign.

We are sitting in a small lounge in Lenasia with two comrades who have been in the struggle for many decades. Both are ex-Robben Islanders; between them they have done over twenty years in prison. Back in 1955 Reggie Vandeyar was 23, and Shirish Nanabhai was just 16.

For Reggie the Congress of the People campaign marked his own increasing and more disciplined involvement in political organisation. He had been actively involved for some years, but by 1955 this involvement was becoming more substantial.

Vandeyar: I was born in 1932, in Newclare. My mum stayed there. But the family moved from pillar to post. I come from a poor family. My dad was from India. The old guy was drawn out here by stories of diamonds, and of gold buried under the streets of Johannesburg. He was into prospecting. He actually carried a little matchbox with him which was supposed to have diamonds in it.

We were a family of nine. By the time of my school-days, when I was a kid of six or seven, we finally settled in Fordsburg. I mixed with a lot of coloured, Indian and African kids. There were Afrikaner kids around too.

We were very hard up in those days. My mother worked at the laundry, for a bob (you know, a shilling) a day. I had to go and collect the shilling before my mother had finished work. It was my task to do the shopping.

She'd send me with a tickey to go buy coal. This Chinese chap sold tins of coal for a tickey. Instead, to have bioscope fare for myself, I used to go to the railway line. I had this pushcart. I'd load the pushcart with spilt coal.

Q: So you used to keep the tickeys for yourself?

Vandeyar: Ja, that type of thing! I was a bit of a drug pusher, too. These were the war years. The laundry man my mother worked for would take me with his horse and cart to the Crown Mines Camp. The soldiers would give me a shilling for a dagga pill. I would make sixpence on a pill! Quite innocently! I did not know there was any danger in carrying this type of stuff.

I did not complete my schooling. I left in standard five during the war years. In those years, I was hanging around. There were four of us. Some of them were to become very prominent in the Congress movement. One was Paul Joseph, he's in London now. And there was the late Barney Desai. Moving around we would sometimes swim at the Blue Dam near Crown Mines. But the Afrikaner boys gave us a hard time. They would beat us up. Or, we would swim naked in the water, right? These guys would take our clothing and burn it, actually burn it.

One time we had to run to Grosvenor station in Mayfair with nothing on but gum-tree leaves! We boarded the train without tickets. Fortunately the conductor did not come around and it is a short distance from Grosvenor to Braamfontein station. We jumped off at Braamfontein and ran home.

We decided we must look for somewhere else to swim. Barney Desai tells us, look, there is the Bantu Social Centre in Wemmer. There is a swimming pool, you can swim free.

They had a library there, called Jubilee Library. We started messing around in the library also. Not really interested in reading. I remember my first book was Daniel Defoe...I can't remember the name offhand. But the interest there was because it was about a prostitute, had some interesting things for a young chap.

Anyway, one day, sitting at the Jubilee Library, an older chap walks in, an acquaintance from Fordsburg. He says: "What are you guys doing in the library? You guys are not ones for this sort of thing." He was ragging us.

So we asked him: "Have you got any money on you?"

"Why do you want money?" he asks.

"We are hungry, to buy some chips."

So he says: "Look man, go to Chancellor House. There is a meeting on there, and they give you fellows tasks to do — collecting silver paper for the war effort — and they'll give you sandwiches and coffee." He took us along.

Chancellor House turned out to be the offices of the Communist Party! After coffee and sandwiches we went out distributing leaflets on the war effort. When we got back in the evening they sent us into another room. It was a Young Communist League speaker. And we sat through the lecture. It was helluva boring! [Laughter.] But that was the beginning of my involvement. ■

For Shirish, also then living in Fordsburg, the path to the struggle was slightly different.

Nanabhai: In a way I would say I was born into the

7

struggle. My dad was involved in politics from his early years. He was in the leadership of the Transvaal Indian Congress. Prior to that even, he had been in the national struggle in India, in the Congress movement there.

There were always discussions going on in our flat. I remember Dr Naicker, Dr Yusuf Dadoo, being there. Walter Sisulu, J.B. Marks, they were always around at home.

Then again our flat was in a fortunate position. We were just across the road from what was normally referred to as 'Red Square'. It was where the Plaza is today. They used to have thousands regularly at huge rallies in Red Square.

Towards the end of 1954, or early part of 1955 I was recruited as an activist. I was 16 then. I got involved in the middle of the Congress of the People campaign, with leaflet distribution and so forth.

Reggie Vandeyar: "We sat through a Young Communist League lecture. It was helluva boring! (laughter). But that was the beginning of my involvement."

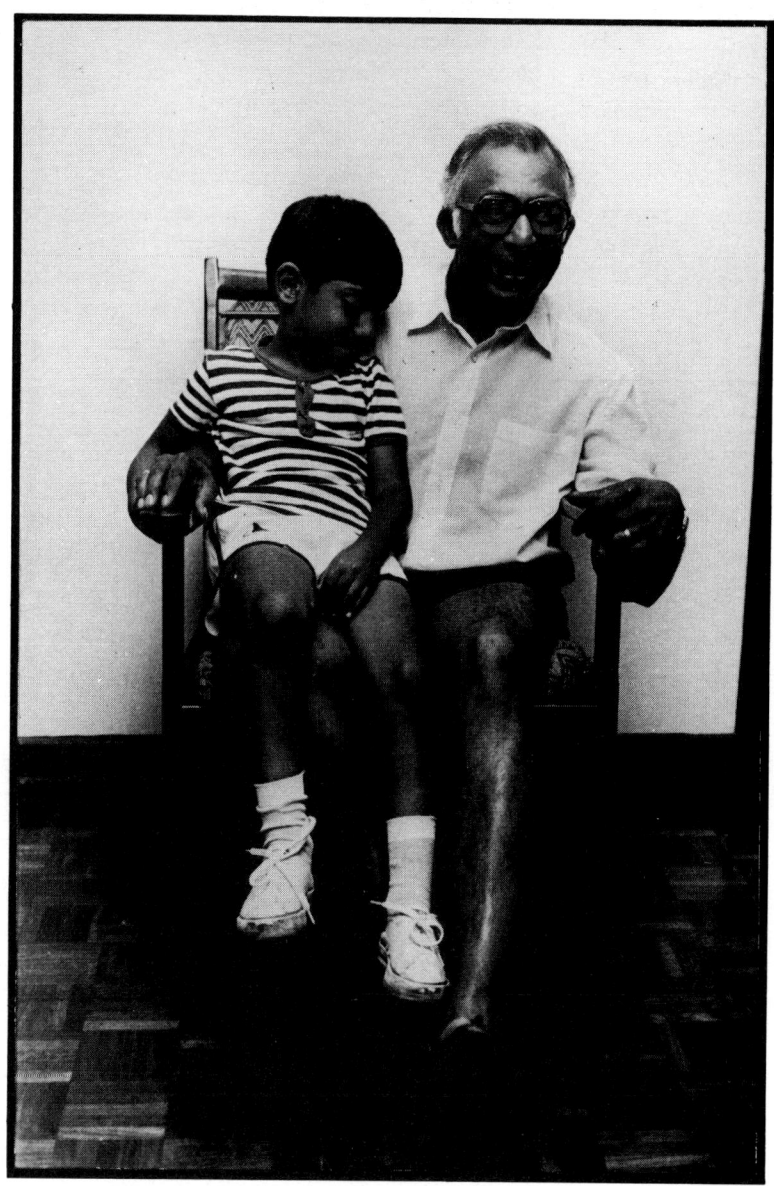

Shirish Nanabhai comes from a family whose involvement in politics stretches back to the national struggle in India: "In a way I would say I was born into the struggle."

Professor Z. K. Matthews formally proposed the idea of a Congress of the People.

II.
The volunteers

4. "An organiser of the people"

Ten thousand volunteers carried the Freedom Charter campaign into the homes, factories, compounds, farms and villages of South Africa.

"Whenever we went to people's houses, and they were in trouble, or had problems, we should become mothers of that family, and men volunteers should be fathers." — Mrs Sibanda, an old Congress of the People volunteer in Cradock.

The idea of a Congress of the People to draw up a document of people's demands had been discussed, off and on, for some years in Congress circles. In August 1953, at the annual Congress of the African National Congress (ANC) (Cape), Prof Z.K. Matthews formally suggested convening a Congress of the People to draw up a Freedom Charter. The idea was soon adopted by the ANC and welcomed by its allies, the South African Indian Congress, the South African Coloured People's Organisation and the South African Congress of Democrats.

The Congress of the People was not a single event but a series of campaigns held in huge rallies, small houses, flats, street and factory meetings, gatherings in kraals and on farms. No doubt the degree of success attained was uneven, yet South Africa has never had any other similar process of democratic discussion and participation.

In March 1954 a National Action Council was established to carry out the campaign. Its job was to gather the people's demands from branches of the various organisations and from communities where there were no branches, and finally, to convene a mass assembly.

The National Action Council called for Freedom Volunteers to serve as 'shock brigades' to give impetus to the campaign. In reply to this call men and women all over South Africa offered their services. The task of these volunteers was to collect the people's demands for the Freedom Charter. How were volunteers to conduct themselves? Were they trained for their tasks? What difficulties did they experience?

We asked many people all over South Africa who were volunteers in the campaign. They gave us a very rich picture. In Port Elizabeth, particularly, the volunteer corps was well organised. We spoke to an old man in Kwazakele township.

Veteran: Oh, well I have to go back right to 1952 now. Because the Freedom Charter campaign was in 1955. The volunteer corps was first set up for volunteers to defy unjust laws.

I was one of the first volunteers, I and Raymond Mhlaba, that registered their names. The volunteers were the people who were prepared to sacrifice on behalf of the liberation movement. The volunteers registered their names, and they were to sacrifice without being paid. They were to suffer, losing their jobs in some cases, because when you defy a law you are due to be arrested. You are now not to fine [bail] yourself. You must serve your prison term out no matter how long. Some of these volunteers lost their jobs through that.

The volunteers had a pledge of discipline which they had to swear that: "I, so-and-so, am prepared to take up on my shoulders the risk of my life for my

Martin Mafefo Ramokgadi dressed in his old volunteer's uniform: "I was a volunteer.... A volunteer had to be simple and sincere."

people, for the liberation struggle. I will do as my leaders tell me. I won't do anything which I have not been instructed to, no matter how the consequences may be."

In the Defiance Campaign, I led my batch of 20, of boys and girls, to defy the apartheid on the railway station of New Brighton. There is a bridge which runs from the Grahamstown road to the station. It has two passages, the one passage for Europeans, the other passage for Africans. The first volunteer that started the Defiance Campaign on that passage of the Europeans, as first volunteer that led a batch of 20 was Raymond Mhlaba. Then it was Samson Ntunja, and then it was me with another batch of 20. ■

The volunteer corps built up in this way during the Defiance Campaign in 1952 and 1953 was to form the backbone of the Congress of the People campaign two years later.

Martin Mafefo Ramokgadi was one of those who went to jail as a volunteer for defying apartheid laws. In the Congress of the People he was again a volunteer. This time the task was to collect demands.

Ramokgadi: From the outset we wanted the campaign to spread all over, towns and countryside — to become a strong movement. I was a volunteer. I collected demands in the urban areas: East Rand, West Rand, Benoni, Springs, Krugersdorp, Sophiatown, Sharpeville.

We always tried to go to areas where the ANC was a bit weak, where membership was not so strong. A volunteer had to be simple and sincere. We must listen. We want people to tell us. ■

In Cape Town, Christmas Fihla Tinto (known as Com T — Comrade Tinto — for short) was elected Volunteer in Chief of the Langa branch of the ANC in 1955.

Tinto: My task was for the disciplinary control of all volunteers for the area, which were the youth of the area. The volunteers of the Defiance Campaign were the same volunteers of the Congress of the People campaign.

They were sometimes elected for certain occasions. For instance, at Langa, if I remember well, I had 145 volunteers. In such occasions as the Defiance Campaign about 30 volunteers were sometimes elected to go to such a duty. In Guguletu, 40. In Nyanga, 50. They came together to be volunteers of that particular campaign.

The volunteers wore khaki uniforms, with a white shirt. It was a policy of discipline. Volunteers were the group of disciplined people who, besides their campaign duties, must keep [Com T gives a big smile] LAW and ORDER, as Le Grange puts it today. ■

A veteran from Port Elizabeth explains the qualities that were looked for in volunteers:

Veteran: *iVolontiya* is a person who actually takes the initiative. A person responsible for talking to people, who knows how to speak to people, what they feel. *Amavolontiya* were trained to behave in a certain way when they meet with people. They are persons who are dedicated to do the work of the organisation, unsupervised. ■

Wilson Fanti, today a community leader at Mgwali outside Stutterheim, was a volunteer in Port Elizabeth. He remembers the training that was

given to volunteers:
Fanti: In Port Elizabeth the volunteers were lectured before they were sent out. They were lectured on how to approach people. First of all, a volunteer was supposed to sign a form that he is a volunteer.

Then volunteers were told about personal appearance. It must be a person who can be accepted by the people. Not a *tsotsi,* or that kind, you see. Not to say he must be highly dressed or something.

Then when they approach the people they must not just start the business. They must first explain their duty, who they are, where they are from and what was the purpose of being here. Then, now they are listened to by the people, they must teach what they are supposed to teach. ∎

The volunteer corps that was trained in Port Elizabeth in this way was to be used to collect demands not just in the Port Elizabeth area, but also in all the rural areas of the Eastern Cape, Ciskei and Transkei. Wilson Fanti even remembers volunteers from Port Elizabeth being sent to the far northern Transvaal, to Sekhukuniland, to collect demands.

Q: To Sekhukuniland? But why from Port Elizabeth?
Fanti: Yes, even to Sekhukuniland. Port Elizabeth was a very strong place. There was the strong leadership of people like the comrade in prison — Comrade Mbeki, and of Dr James Njongwe, and Raymond [Mhlaba] also now in jail. Even Walter Sisulu used to go down to Port Elizabeth to give lectures.

That is why Port Elizabeth catch up so well! ∎

But it was not just in Port Elizabeth that a strong corps of volunteers was built. In Pietermaritzburg, A.S. Chetty also remembers volunteers receiving training for the Congress of the People campaign.
Chetty: We were taught as volunteers, we used to have regular classes to say how we must go about interviewing people. Simplicity, and manners, and all those kind of things.

And I tell you it brought out the best qualities in our fellows, because we had a group of very dedicated chaps. They'd get up very early in the morning, they didn't eat breakfast or anything of the sort. Wear your khaki safari, and charge along. Then come three or four o'clock in the afternoon, we would meet at some assembly point and discuss what we had done. ∎

Reggie Vandeyar was living in Fordsburg at that time. He recalls the activities of volunteers from the Transvaal Indian Congress.
Vandeyar: Most of the campaigning was done over weekends. At times individuals would say they've got time during the week. Fordsburg, Jeppe, Doornfontein, Vrededorp, Malay Camp — these areas could be covered during the weekdays as well. But we had very few activists in places like Pretoria and Benoni, Nigel, Springs. Activists in the Johannesburg central area would organise groups to go out into these areas.

Weekends we would gather, say, twenty activists in the Indian Congress offices, and we would split up in groups of, say, five. Five to Pretoria, five here, five there. We would go out with African, coloured and white comrades. ∎

On the basis of the volunteer corps that had

developed in the Defiance Campaign, and recruiting many thousands more, a team of 10 000 volunteers was built up all over South Africa. The preparation of volunteers was, perhaps, not always as thorough in some centres as it was in others. But the same dedication and spirit of sacrifice was found everywhere.

For many volunteers the collection of demands provided their first opportunity to go into the homes of people whose background and customs were very different from their own. For many volunteers, catching trains and then going miles and miles on foot, the campaign revealed to them the conditions out in the rural areas. While the people were to learn from the volunteers, the volunteers were also learning from the people.

"iVoluntiya is a person who actually takes initiative"

5. Document: "To all volunteers"

This circular written in January 1955 stresses the need for volunteers to work with and listen carefully to ordinary people.

Dear Volunteer

Greetings to you for the New Year. It will be a good year — a year of success for our Congress of the People — if we get down to work without delay.

By decision of the National Council, the Congress of the People will definitely be called before June of this year. There is a great deal to do before you can say "Now we are ready; the people are ready; our Congress of the People will be a tremendous success."

What are the things we need to do?

First: We must collect in the demands of the people for inclusion in the Freedom Charter. This work must start **now**; by 30th [sic] of February, 1955, we must have received the claims and demands of the people, so that the work of assembling all these demands into a single Charter can go ahead.

WHAT IS THE FREEDOM CHARTER?

The Freedom Charter will be the Charter of the demands of all the South African people for the things that they want to make their lives happy and free. It will be a document to guide all our future work, but it will be written by the ordinary people themselves, through the demands that they themselves send in. It is hoped that thousands and thousands of gatherings, some small, some large, will be held where people can speak freely of their own lives, what changes they want in their way of life, in the laws they live under and in the conditions. Look at the — "Call" — in it are the kinds of things that people will talk about — the land, wages, taxes, education, health, recreation, laws, food and peace. From these meetings, no matter how small they are, will come the demands of the people for the changes they want. All these demands, no matter how trifling, no matter how local they may be — **ALL** those demands of the people must be noted on, recorded and sent in for inclusion in the Freedom Charter. And they must be in by not later than the 28th February, 1955.

When all these demands are received, they will be put together, carefully, to make a single Charter which will truly be the voice of the people of this country. And this Charter — the Freedom Charter — will then be put to the elected delegates of the nation at the Congress of the People, so that they can dilute it, discuss it and adopt it as a guide for all who wish for and work for Freedom.

WHAT MUST A FREEDOM VOLUNTEER DO?

A volunteer is an organiser and a leader of the people. Now, in the next two months — but starting right away now without delay — he must organise people to formulate their demands. We must call people together, explain to them the Freedom Charter, encourage them to speak out, listen to their demands, and record their demands and send them in to the Congress of the People Committee. For some volunteers a start can be made in their own factories or their own place of work — where lunch-hour discussion with his work-mates can be arranged. For all volunteers, a meeting of neighbours in a house, perhaps only of one street or block, can be called together. From these small beginnings we must branch off, going from street to street, from block to block, organising meetings, explaining, listening, recording. For the next few months, volunteers must work like missionaries, without resting. It should be one's aim to meet with one group of people or another every night, systematically covering our whole town or locality so that no citizen of South Africa is left out of the discussions on the Freedom Charter.

This is a big task — a tremendous task. But a good volunteer does not work alone! He works in the first place with the other volunteers in the neighbourhood, planning together with them all that is to be done. But even when a volunteer starts to work alone, with no other to assist him, his task is — at every meeting — to call on those who are inspired by the ideals of the Freedom Charter to take their own initiative — to call their own meetings — in their own places of work and to become also organisers and leaders for the Freedom Charter.

Let us not overlook the countryside. Volunteers from the towns who have relations and families in the countryside must try to get to the rural areas on the week-ends, and hold discussions on the Charter. They must urge, at every meeting in the towns that all the people write or visit their friends in the rural areas and in the villages, to tell them about the Freedom Charter, and to urge them to make their demands without delay. Everyone who has made his own demand must now organise others to do the same! Let the Freedom Charter spread like wild fire among the people.

HOW SHOULD A MEETING BE CONDUCTED?

At every meeting the volunteer should start by explaining the Congress of the People. They should explain that the African National Congress, South African Indian Congress, South African Congress of Democrats and the South African Coloured People's Organisation have joined hands to call elected representatives of the people to a central assembly — THE CONGRESS OF THE PEOPLE — not later than June of this year. They should explain that at this assembly the Freedom Charter will be adopted. They should explain that the Freedom Charter is to be written by the people everywhere in small and great gatherings, who will voice their own demands and send their demands in for inclusion in the Charter.

The "Call" to the Congress of the People should then be read. Volunteers should explain that the time has now come for the people at the meeting to speak together — to speak of Freedom and of what it means for them.

The volunteers should carefully write down the demands and grievances that are voiced. They should guide the discussion so that people do not only say what they suffer from but also what changes must be made to set things right. They must encourage people to talk of small things, and not speak generally of 'unjust laws' or 'oppression'. They must ask — what laws are unjust, and what should be done about them; what is oppression, and how it can be abolished.

At the end of the meeting, all the demands of the people should then be read out by the volunteers, and the meeting asked to vote for or against their inclusion in the Freedom Charter. The people at the meeting should be asked to discuss their demands. The meeting should be asked to appoint a Committee for the Congress of the People, which will carry on the work in the area, and which will prepare to organise and hold elections for a delegate of the people to go to the Congress of the People when the call is given. But the volunteer's tasks do not end with the meeting. After the meeting he must see that the report form is filled in, that all demands of the people are written on the report and that the report is handed in to the local Congress of the People Committee, or posted to the National Action Council at Post Office Box 11045, Johannesburg.

This is a great task. But freedom is not easily won! It is won through hard, persistent work, organising the people, mobilising them and leading them forward.

LET'S GET DOWN TO IT **NOW**, WITHOUT DELAY.

Yours for Freedom,

NATIONAL ACTION COUNCIL

6. Document: "Listen young friend"

A great deal of literature was distributed during the Congress of the People campaign. It was directed at the people in general but also aimed at particular groupings. This pamphlet addressed Indian youth.

Listen friend...

Yes it's you I mean — Amrit, Amina, Marimoothu, or whatever your name is — what are you interested in? Football? Cricket? Swimming, maybe, or other sports? What are you keen on? Films? Dancing? Studying, perhaps? Do you like reading? Do you want a chance to learn a proper trade or profession?

Whatever it is, there are thousands like you, young South Africans who never have the chance to get the kind of education they should, who are prevented from using their skills and talents to the full, who are frustrated in their search for decent employment and restricted in their leisure-time activities by the absence of sports and cultural amenities.

Every young person born in this country is entitled to certain things, no matter who he is or what his race.

Why shouldn't you get them? Why shouldn't you have a chance to go to good, well-equipped schools? To enjoy playing fields and sports equipment? Swimming baths, recreation centres, libraries? Why shouldn't you have a chance to study to the fullest of your ability, and a chance to practise the trade or job or profession of your choice?

Millions of South Africans are asking these same questions today and are determined to do something about it, too. Unless your are prepared to sit down and submit to harsh indignities and discrimination, *you* should do something about it as well.

Millions of South Africans during the coming weeks and months are going to discuss what they want from life, what they think they are entitled to, what they understand by freedom. They are going to speak of freedom, and draw up their demands into a Freedom Charter. And of all the demands, those that affect the youth are most important, because it's you, and all the young people like you, with the best part of their lives in front of them, who will enjoy that freedom so long denied to most South Africans.

Speak together of freedom!

A call has gone out to the people of South Africa to speak together of freedom. The call was drawn up by four organisations, representing the different sections of South Africans — African National Congress, the South African Indian Congress, the Congress of Democrats and the South African Coloured People's Organisation.

It is a call for a greater assembly of elected representatives of all races, from town and countryside, from city and farm, from factory and mine, from street and kraal, to meet together, freely, as equals, and speak of the changes that must be made in our lives, our laws, our customs, our outlooks, if we are to win freedom for the people of South Africa.

Most South Africans have never voted in an election. This will be an assembly of elected delegates, who will draw up the demands of all the people into the FREEDOM CHARTER.

Into this Charter will go the things you ought to have, the things you want and need. The Freedom Charter will be a living document, breathing the life of the people of this country.

How can such a mighty Congress be organised? Only through a band of voluntary helpers, who will cover the country from end to end, who will enter every town and village, who will go into every factory, every place where people work.

These people will be FREEDOM VOLUNTEERS, pledged to carry to every corner of the country the message of the Congress of the People, and to gather in the demands of the people for the Freedom Charter.

This is the most inspiring, most exciting task that any young person of this country can undertake.

It is a job, for you, Ahmed, Ismail, or whatever your name is. Don't sit back and dream of what you would like from life. Write your hopes into the Freedom Charter!

Become a Freedom Volunteer!

What is required of a Freedom Volunteer? You are not being asked to give up your job or leave your studies. You will pledge yourself to undertake regular, active and intensive work for the Congress of the People, and for resistance to the Apartheid policy of the Government.

You will be asked to take a pledge to serve your country and your people to the best of your ability, and in accordance with the policy and programme of the organisation to which you belong.

You will be asked to study the political and economic life of our country, and classes will be organised for that study.

You will be asked to assist in any tasks related to the Congress of the People, particularly with bringing news of the Congress to other people.

Your age is not important. Freedom Volunteers will be organised into units under a leader, and boys and girls under sixteen will have separate groups.

A call has gone out for 50,000 voluteers. These 50,000 people will be the backbone of the whole campaign — on their shoulders will rest the success of the Congress of the People.

FILL IN THIS FORM — NOW!

LISTEN YOUNG FRIEND

TURN THE PAGE. IT'S YOUR LIFE WE'RE DISCUSSING . . . AND YOUR'E THE ONE WHO CAN DO SOMETHING ABOUT IT.

FILL IN THIS FORM — NOW!

Send it off to this address, or take it to your organisation — today.

CONGRESS OF THE PEOPLE
Box 11045
Johannesburg

CONGRESS OF THE PEOPLE
Box 2299
Durban

I would like to become a Freedom Volunteer. Please tell me how to enrol.

NAME ....

ADDRESS ....
....
....

This pamphlet was issued by the South African Indian Youth Congress calling for volunteers.

III.
Collecting demands

7. "A two card carrying member"

In the words of 'Com T' we hear how demands were collected in the factories during the day and in the Cape Town townships at night.

We have already met Com T, once the Volunteer in Chief for Langa. Christmas Fihla Tinto is today vice-chairperson of the UDF (Western Cape). He always wears a big smile. Perhaps it is because he has been sentenced twice to long spells of prison, and twice, after some time on Robben Island, he has got off on appeal. Maybe he smiles because of his luck, maybe he has been smiling ever since he was born in the festive season, Christmas Day 1925.

Com T grew up in the Transkei, and then worked as a contract labourer on the mines. After being involved in a strike he was blacklisted. So, in the early 1950s, he came to Cape Town to look for work. He soon became involved in union organising.

Tinto: In 1954 I organised a hospital workers' union in five months. Thereafter I was instructed by the movement, by the ANC, to organise the railways, because at the railways are mostly people coming from rural areas. They speak deep Xhosa, just like myself. You were told in those times to go and do that. You don't say that I do what I think. You do what you are told to.

Still in 1954 then, I went to organise the railways. I went to Johannesburg to get training there, on how to approach the problems involved there. I met the comrade, the late Lawrence Ndzanga there. We discussed together. Although I heard that Joshua

Nkomo was organising the railway workers as well in Pietermaritzburg I couldn't get a chance to go there. Then I was involved in the Railway Workers Union till I was detained in 1963 under 90-days detention.

Q: Was it very difficult to get access to the railway workers?

Tinto: Ja. It was. But we used various tactics. For instance, if you are organising an industry you must have a *uniform* of that particular industry. The first thing I bought a railway overall, when I go inside the gate the watchman, the police whoever, he doesn't differentiate from these other people. I just went inside. Usually I used to go closer lunch time, so that at lunch I addressed them in the mess-room.

Q: Did you collect demands from railway workers in this way during the Congress of the People campaign?

Tinto: Yes. Ja, that's right.

Q: Did the workers ever betray you?

Tinto: No. Another thing, as I said earlier, all ANC members were to form trade unions in those industries where they were working. When I go to a work-place, even if I don't know it, I see someone coming closer to me.

I say: [in a low voice] "Yes, comrade, I'm comrade so-and-so, I'm staying in so-and-so."

"O, ja. What is your problem?"

"I have come to address a meeting."

"Okay, comrade, it's alright" or "Don't come today, come tomorrow so I will announce it, that everybody will be here."

[All this in a low voice.]

I mean to say that we got the help of the comrades working in these different industries.

Christmas Tinto ('Com T'), Volunteer in Chief in Langa: "Volunteers must keep LAW and ORDER, as Le Grange puts it today."

Q: In collecting demands from railway workers, did you speak to them individually as well as in groups?
Tinto: No. Mainly in groups. To those who were asking, perhaps after the meeting, as the time is short at lunchtime. People were asking questions till such time as the bell rings, two o'clock, must go to work again. Some even come to my house to ask for clarification.
Q: Comrade Billy Nair has told us that in Natal every single factory, even Tucsa factories, were reached in the Congress of the People campaign. How did things go in the Western Cape?
Tinto: Ja, Billy, it is true what he said. Natal was well organised in the trade union scene. It was more uneven in other places.
Q: Here in Cape Town was Sactu [the South African Congress of Trade Unions] strong among coloured workers?
Tinto: It was strong among the African workers. But Sactu was not so developed. The reason — Africans are in small numbers here in Cape Town, unlike in Natal and Transvaal. ∎

Com T's work in the Congress of the People campaign was not confined to collecting demands from workers at their places of work.
Tinto: The policy of the ANC was that a *comrade must be a two card carrying member of the struggle.* You must have a card of Sactu, of a trade union, and you must have a card of a national oppression. ANC and Sactu both. When I come home from work I get on with the work of the ANC in the township. Ja. Both. ∎

In Langa township, where Com T was Volunteer-in-Chief, the task was to go house to house, to collect demands from the widest range of people.
Tinto: Even the witchdoctors. I remember I went to a house in which witchdoctors were planning their celebration there. We talked to them (I was going with another comrade). They said that their demand is that the government must give them the halls where to dance as witchdoctors. They must have a right to halls, they must have their hospitals where they keep their patients and cure them. That, we wrote it down because it was said whatever section of the people ...we must take down their demands.
Q: And traders?
Tinto: There was a shopkeeper at Bunga Square at Langa. That shopkeeper, I remember, he demanded that we must have shops in Cape Town where people are, where we choose to have our shops. I mean such things.

But most people made demands to have political rights. Though some couldn't mention what kind of political rights. They say political rights to elect our people to go to parliament.

In the Western Cape, I was a voter myself. We used to vote for the liberals, and people like Sam Kahn, Communist Party people.

Now the government cancelled that vote because if today Sam Kahn, a member of the Communist Party, is going to have a public meeting canvassing for election in Langa area, now the hall is going to be full, even outside. But, next week, a member of the Nationalist Party, Tom Donges, is going to address the meeting at Langa Hall, nobody will attend that meeting.

Now, the government get angry to that, and he cut off our voting rights.

Q: What happened when you went to a house?
Tinto: Mother and father, you sit here. You talk to them.
Q: What did you say?
Tinto: There is a Congress of the People which is coming, which needs everybody to voice out his or her opinion as to what, how does she see this country to look like.

If I come to this house, I call those next door to come here. To do the talking to a small group.

Q: Was this to save time?
Tinto: You know there are some people, who they know they are oppressed but they don't know what to do. When you ask him: "What do you think?" he'll say: "Why, I don't know. I'm a black man. I've got nothing."

But if someone hears from someone, he or she can say this and this and this. Now something slides from his or her mind that I can as well bring this up.
Q: So it was a way of getting fuller participation?
Tinto: Ja. *That's* right. ∎

Wilson Fanti happened to be staying for a while in Langa at that time. He was one of those whose homes were visited by Com T's Congress of the People volunteers.
Fanti: They sat down and explained what they wanted. They spoke about the Frontier Wars, how our people had been defeated and their land taken away. They explained the beginning of the ANC in 1912.

Then they wanted to know from us the type of government if South Africa could be free. They asked us to put our views. For example, one gentleman which was residing with me in the same house said that the question of taxes must be abolished. That was *his* suggestion. Such were the views collected. ∎

We asked Com T if people sometimes came out with demands that he thought were reactionary.
Tinto: Hmm, mmh. I would like to tell you a story.... I remember on the Island when black consciousness came there in big numbers from the Eastern Cape. Comrades from Pietermaritzburg were shocked, but we said to them, don't forget even the Nelson Mandela of today was once like those youngsters. Black consciousness, we said, it is a first stage of political awareness. They see the structure of South Africa as it is. It is your duty now to go further, to explain to them that's not the end of the road. They must go further.

Now, why I say this, uh, even there in 1955 there were people who were saying: "Ja, I will agree if we are going to chase the white people away from this country." Talking that type of language. We didn't call them reactionary as such. Ja, no.

Q: So did you write down such demands, like driving out the whites?
Tinto: I write it down. But I would ask them how they thought such a thing could help...trying to get them to understand better.

But the people say: "These people, can't you see that they are oppressing us? We have got no houses. We have got nothing. We have no money.... But we are told that our grandfathers were happy, living nicely without the white people, before they arrived here."

Then I write those reasons as well. ∎

Apart from house to house work, area meetings

were also held in Langa, to popularise the Congress of the People campaign and to collect demands.

Tinto: We go round by loudspeaker: "There's a meeting in Bunga Square! All must come!" I put up a table like this kitchen table. And there's a stand like this. So that whoever is going to speak must be seen by everybody in the open air.

Q: Did you collect demands at these big meetings as well?

Tinto: That's right.

Q: How many would be at a meeting like that?

Tinto: Some, a thousand eight hundred to one thousand five hundred.

Q: How would you collect demands?

Tinto: We used to have a certain table. After we have explained to them, there was a certain table. All those who have got their demands must go to that table. We still continued talking.

A large workforce was required to collect demands across the length and breadth of the country. This pamphlet calls for Freedom Volunteers. The Congress of the People organisers recruited 10 000 volunteers.

WHY HAVE YOU NOT VOLUNTEERED?

8. Cradock, the cradle of the Charter

From Cradock, where 32 years ago the idea of a Freedom Charter was first formally proposed, Mrs Sibanda and Mrs Calata recall collecting demands.

Two hundred and sixty kilometres north of Port Elizabeth is the small Karroo *dorp* of Cradock. Despite its isolation Cradock has a long history of struggle. To this day the people in Cradock's township maintain their militant tradition.

Thirty-two years back, in August 1953, the ANC (Cape) held its annual conference in Cradock. It was at this conference that it was resolved to send forward to the ANC National Executive the idea of a Congress of the People, and a Freedom Charter. The rest is history....

Out here now, in Cradock's dusty township, Mrs Sibanda and Mrs Calata both remember those times well. In the 1950s Mrs Sibanda was very active in the ANC Women's League and in the Federation of South African Women. Mrs Calata is the daughter of the late ANC leader, Canon James A. Calata. She was also in the Women's League, but her main involvement was in her father's famous Congress Choir.

Q: Mrs Sibanda, were you here in Cradock in 1955?
Sibanda: I was here.
Q: Do you remember this campaign to get demands for the Freedom Charter?
Sibanda: I was one of the people who collected

demands. But we felt that before we did that, we should go and defy the laws. The demands of the people at that time were this question of passes, and not being allowed to go out at night. ■

The historical records show that in Cradock no fewer than 53 volunteers were arrested for defying unjust laws like the curfew.

Q: When you collected demands did you write them down?

Sibanda: Well, volunteers would go and discuss the conditions under which people lived, and as people voiced out their grievances, the volunteers would write them down.

Q: Were there women volunteers? Did women play a part in this campaign?

Sibanda: Yes. The women were very strong here in Cradock. We used to be arrested! ■

Conditions in the countryside were often much worse than in the towns. When we asked old volunteers in the towns if they ever had difficulties, most said there were no major problems, but there were sometimes people who were rude, or who refused to cooperate. When Mrs Sibanda was asked this question about difficulties encountered in a rural area like Cradock, she had a very different answer.

Sibanda: We used to have problems, because, let's say we visited a house, there's a man there, and there's no food whatsoever. In some cases we would find people who were very sick. One day we met an old man who was from the countryside, a bit away from Cradock. He had been expelled from a white farm, and he had the corpse of his child with him on the road. We took this child to our Rev. Calata, and he buried him. He used to collect people even from the outskirts, and bury them, and then he would be called by the magistrate to give an account of why he did that.

Rev. Calata's teaching to us was that whenever we went to people's houses, and they were in trouble, or had problems, we should become mothers of that family, and men volunteers should be fathers.

Q: Did the volunteers also go out to farms and farm-workers around Cradock?

Calata: It was not easy for them to do that because the Dutch people were very aggressive, very aggressive. But they did try. The farmers didn't like their servants to be disturbed. Even if my father went to give a church service, they would call the workers while the service was going on: "Kom Piet, kom werk nou." [Come Piet, come and work now.]

Q: What were the problems people were raising when you collected demands here in Cradock itself?

Sibanda: One of our problems was water — we didn't have taps in the location, we had to walk to town to fetch water. It would take almost the whole day. There were some drums, and we had to wait in a very long queue. Another difficulty was sometimes we would go and collect wood, and we'd be stopped. They would take the wood to the police station and we would be fined for that. Also, our houses were made of zinc. We had no money for materials to build houses. Also there were no toilets.

Q: Were there any grievances in relation to education?

Sibanda: We did have grievances about education. Children had to wear uniforms bought by their parents, they had to have books bought by their parents, and school fees had to be paid, and even bibles had to be bought by parents. We could just not afford to buy books because of the low wages.

Calata: There were very few lavatories in people's yards — there were public lavatories which were not kept clean. When we appealed to the authorities, it would be said: "It is still under consideration".

Here in Cradock, there were nurses who, though they were qualified, they couldn't work in the clinic. It had to be a white lady. We thought these people who have been trained could be working here for their own people, at the location. When that was voiced out, the whites said it was 'politics'.

So a lot of things were unworthy. I shall just speak about Cradock — Cradock was rather poorer than other places. Now, when the ANC was in motion here, then people used to go to their meetings. So they had their meetings, everyone had to voice out his or her grievances. They had to write all these grievances down.

They discussed these things, and then there would be conferences where they met other people from all the places. Conditions would be more or less the same. They thought then that this must be rectified in some way or other. I should think that's how the Freedom Charter was formed. Because it includes a lot of things that were irritating the people.

Calata: This was so bad that not many people could afford to have their children at school in Cradock, until these ANC people said there must be a way to help. Then it was that Rev. Calata's Congress Choir aimed to raise funds, and paid for those children even until they got up to JC [Junior Certificate — Standard Eight]. This choir was raising funds for the ANC — that was why it was called the Congress Choir. My father helped a lot of children here in Cradock.

Q: Was there any organisation in the coloured area in Cradock?

Calata: The coloureds didn't have any organisation. At that time, the coloureds were part of the location. There was no Michausdal [present coloured township in Cradock]. We were divided only in 1969. I remember in our streets we were just mixed.

Sibanda: At that time we were speaking Afrikaans. I used to play with the coloured children. I really used to speak Afrikaans like anything!

Calata: Now we are divided into separate Group Areas, but the Freedom Charter doesn't like these discriminatory laws.

Sibanda: The people who must govern are the people. The black people because they are the majority. There must not be this *baasskap*. We must end this *baasskap* because it does not mean anything. It just means oppression, that is all. And the Freedom Charter demands equal rights, for every person, whatever race or creed. I think the Charter's very much important and it's still relevant today.

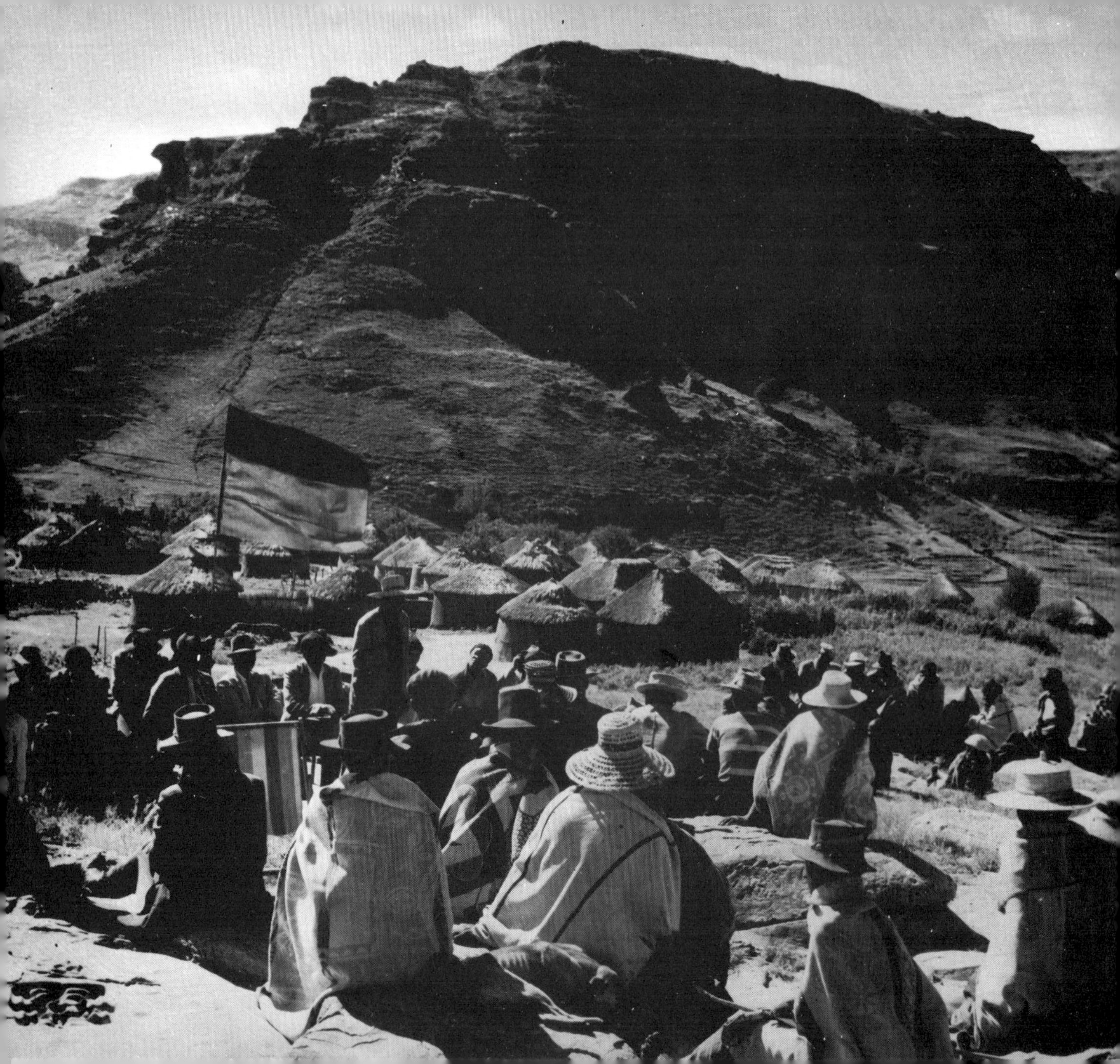

9. "The first question was the land"

Wilson Fanti and Edgar Ngoyi recall the tough but rewarding times they had collecting demands in the rural areas of the Border and Transkei.

By road Stutterheim is about 100 kilometres to the north-west of East London. Another 30 kilometres in the direction of Transkei brings you to the settlement of Mgwali. Mgwali dates back to the 1850s. It was a mission area, created as a buffer zone in the midst of the Frontier Wars. Like so many other long established settlements, Mgwali is today under threat of removal or forced incorporation into the Ciskei bantustan. Chairperson of the Mgwali Residents' Association and in the forefront of opposition to the threatened removal is Wilson Fanti, the very same Fanti who remembers Com T's volunteers coming to his house in Langa, Cape Town.

At the beginning of the campaign Fanti was, indeed, in Cape Town. Then a few months later he was active as a volunteer in Port Elizabeth. However, throughout the period he remained in contact with his home in Mgwali, and with the Stutterheim district in general.

Fanti: At that time the people of Stutterheim district were very well organised.

Firstly, in Stutterheim there was a big meeting which was held right inside the town. I remember at this meeting it was explained that there would be people going around taking their views, house to house. ■

◀ The Congress Alliance, through its expansion into rural areas, was transformed into a national movement during the Congress of the People campaign. Here is a meeting in the heart of the Maluti mountains.

Edgar Ngoyi, an ex-Robben Islander who recently completed a 17-year prison sentence, is now president of the UDF Eastern Cape region. In 1954-5 he was sent as a volunteer from Port Elizabeth to the rural areas.

Ngoyi: I went to Stutterheim (my home town), Peddie, Kingwilliamstown, and other areas. ■

Wilson Fanti also remembers volunteers from East London being sent to the Stutterheim district.

Fanti: The people of Stutterheim were encouraged by these volunteers to go to Kliptown, and transport was organised for them after their views were collected. Not all the people of Stutterheim went to Kliptown. But their views, including Mgwali, even workers on farms for that matter, were asked. They were asked what type of government they wished.

Q: What sorts of difficulties did volunteers experience in the rural areas?

Fanti: Really, in areas like Transkei and Pondoland it was very difficult to work.

The volunteer would take a long time to find a way of approaching that particular group, or that particular person, or that particular chief. A person coming from outside your area you do not accept unless you have been introduced to him by the chief.

Some of the chiefs were pro-government, they didn't want to accept these things. So in that area you had to seek another means of getting to the people behind the chief.

In the rural areas people do not just catch a thing. You have to take time, to explain a thing. You have to try and try just to get one, a prominent person from that area. Then teach that person. That person, because of his respect with the other people, if this issue is brought by *him*, then people will accept it.

It is true that some of the chiefs were organised in this way to join the struggle. Some of the chiefs in the Transkei, I am not going to mention names, called meetings. Then the issue was explained to the people.

The question of transport was another problem in that time. We didn't have enough money. Some of the volunteers used to travel on foot a long distance. Some decided to stay in the rural areas for quite a long time. Transport was really scarce.

Q: What demands do you remember coming from the rural areas?

Fanti: One of the demands was LAND for the peasants. Those people believe in land for their livestock. Because the land had been taken away from them, the people cannot supply themselves as before. So the first question was the land....

[Wilson Fanti, leader of the Mgwali community under threat of forced removal, clicks his tongue and shakes his head.]

...Yes, that was the first demand, which is STILL a problem today. ■

Edgar Ngoyi remembers another demand coming from the reserves.

Ngoyi: We went to the reserves where we spoke to the peasants. They gave demands for the government to give them tractors. ■

Volunteers also had the difficult task of collecting demands from labourers on white farms.

Fanti: To go to the farms the volunteers had to ask the boss to seek a permission to go in. During that time the farmers were really aware of what was taking place in towns. So we had to answer many questions: "Who are you? Where are you from?" and so forth, and so forth. So we had to disguise what we were doing on the farm.

Ngoyi: When we went to speak to farm-workers, we had to approach the relatives of farm-workers we knew, and so go and speak to the workers. It was difficult to go on to the farms because the farmers didn't want 'clean' people 'spoiling' their farm-workers. 'Clean' people were people from the city. ∎

The work was difficult in the rural areas of Border and Transkei, but Wilson Fanti feels it had a real impact in those times.

Fanti: That's right. Definite. By going out and talking to people the volunteers just put a light in the rural areas.

Wilson Fanti, now chairperson of the Mgwali Residents Association: "The volunteers just put a light in the rural areas."

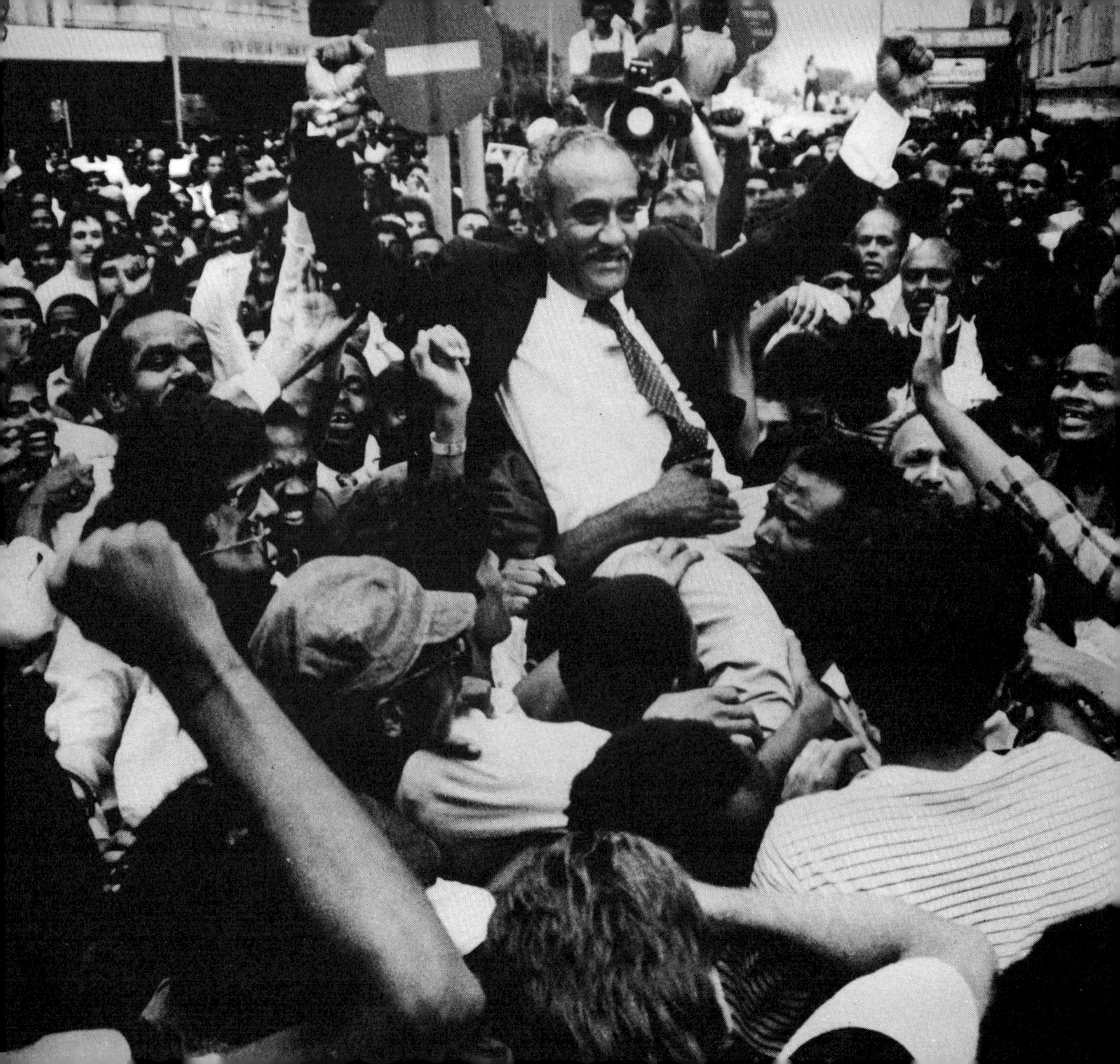

10. The workers' demands

The working class played the leading role in shaping the Freedom Charter. Not only did worker militants collect many of the demands but it was the workers in the factories, mines and farms that were the main source of demands.

◀ Billy Nair was active in Sactu's campaign to collect demands for the Freedom Charter. After 20 years in prison, he is still struggling to achieve its principles. He was one of the six UDF leaders who occupied the British consulate in Durban at the end of 1984 to highlight apartheid repression. This picture is taken after he left the building.

We have already glimpsed at the role of workers and trade union organisation in the Congress of the People campaign. In many centres it was worker militants and union organisers who were the most active volunteers. Those volunteers carried a working-class outlook into the townships and rural areas.

But, at the same time, volunteers often found themselves learning from the experiences of organised workers. Reggie Vandeyar, for instance, particularly remembers the women clothing-workers he met while collecting demands in Johannesburg.

Vandeyar: Eyy, man, those women taught us some things! In the coloured areas of Coronationville, Albertsville, Noordgesig you found women who would be able to come out with a lot of grievances about houses and wages. None of the shyness of women we met in other areas. It was because many of them were factory workers. The Garment Workers' Union was quite a powerful union in those days, with Solly Sachs and Anna Scheepers in the leadership. The coloured women workers would interlink your questions with the demands they were making at work. They would come out and tell us certain things we did not even have in the questionnaire forms — issues of trade unionism, demands for higher wages.

39

In this connection the whole housing problem was interesting. When we approached an individual we would ask them: "Are you satisfied with the area you are living in? Would you like to live in an area like Houghton?"

Now we were trying to *politicise*. To get people to say they were against Group Areas. We were trying to get people to say they would like the right to live in a posh area like Houghton. But those coloured women workers showed us it wasn't just Group Areas. They said: "Houghton? Who can live in Houghton? Who's going to pay so much money?" They were demanding full trade union rights and higher wages. ■

In March 1955, just a few months before the Congress of the People, Sactu was formed. Collecting workers' demands for the Freedom Charter became the special task of Sactu. In fact the Congress of the People campaign was Sactu's first national campaign. The campaign helped to unify the ranks of organised workers within Sactu's federation of progressive trade unions. But it also helped to carry the trade union message to thousands of still unorganised workers.

In many places Sactu organisers seem to have performed the lion's share of the work. Liz Abrahams ('Nana') remembers:

Abrahams: Here in Paarl most of the collecting of demands was done by Sactu people. Sactu leader, Archie Sibeko went round collecting. Sibeko would go from house to house. ■

It is from the Durban area that we have our richest picture of Sactu's activities in the collection of demands. It was here in this city that Billy Nair was born in 1929.

Nair: There were four of us in the family, well five, one brother died young. We came from a very poor lot, I'd say. When all of us passed through primary school my parents were unable to afford high school, and we immediately started work. I found a job as a shop assistant. I worked for 18 shillings and seven pence a week. I saw at first hand the rigours of exploitation — that was 1946. ■

That first experience of exploitation sparked in Billy Nair a lifelong hatred for all forms of oppression. It started him on a long trip, through the stormy years of mass campaigning in the 1950s, into the Treason Trial where he was one of the 156 charged, through the mass stay-aways in the late 1950s and early 1960s. In 1964 Billy Nair was sentenced to 20 years imprisonment on Robben Island. He served that sentence, down to the last day, and he was released in 1984.

The 20 years in prison have in no way dented Billy Nair's commitment to the struggle. Soon after his release he was again being hounded by the police. He made international headlines when along with five others, he occupied the British consulate in Durban.

But let us return to the earlier years of Billy Nair's involvement in the struggle.

Nair: In 1951 I became the secretary of the Dairy Workers' Union. I had just been dismissed from employment: I'd been working as a clerk in the Durban dairies.

At the time the government was trying to smash progressive trade unions. In 1953 there was a spate of banning orders. Suddenly, overnight, I was forced to take on about 16 trade unions — it was just simply impossible! Banning orders were issued against many, many trade unionists, like H.B. Reddy, George Poonen, and many more. They were forced to resign their positions in the trade unions.

So I had, well, a *bit* of training in union work, but not sufficient to man 16 trade unions! [Shaking his head, Billy lets his eyes narrow down to a twinkle.] Ja *boetie*, heh, I was forced to sleep in that office. In fact 'sleep' is hardly the word. I had to work night and day.

Then you had to contend with police raids, and employer harassment. None of our trade unions enjoyed stop-order facilities, or any kind of recognition from the bosses. So you had to hold meetings outside the factory premises, outdoors. The police were forever locking you up, for holding your meetings on public property, and so on. So this was a constant thing. You were appearing in court, pleading guilty, paying some fine. You were repeatedly forced to break the laws.

The Nationalist government made their position quite clear. In the words of Ben Schoeman, Minister of Labour, they were going "to bleed the African trade unions to death".

Despite all this harassment we were able to organise militant trade unions. These unions grouped together nationally to form Sactu. Within Sactu heavy reliance was placed on educating the workers at the factory-floor level.

Now there is, of course, a suggestion by the workerists of today that Sactu was not an organisation of workers but largely a political party. This is in fact not true. Sactu's policy was to build strong union organisation at the shop-floor level, and, where possible, to form industrial unions.

But Sactu also *had* to politicise the workers. Without such politicisation we could not have survived as long as we did. With all the harassment of the police and bosses we needed union members who were highly motivated to belong to trade unions. We needed workers who would be able to *maintain* the union organisation even if the leadership was entirely removed.

Trade unions were to be seen as organisations to assist in the struggle of workers to free themselves from all types of oppression, exploitation of the bosses and oppression by the government. I mean we needed to develop in the worker a fuller class consciousness.

Many outstanding militants came up through the ranks of the Sactu unions, among them my close comrade Curnick Ndlovu. Members of Sactu unions did not think of trade unionism for the mere sake of it, merely to gain higher wages and better working conditions; the very question of class rule itself had to be tackled.

It was this kind of thinking that led Sactu to throw its full weight behind the Congress of the People campaign. Sactu, and the working class at large, participated actively in drawing up the Freedom Charter.

Q: Billy, how exactly were demands for the Freedom Charter collected from workers?
Nair: From *Sactu's* point of view, from the time of its formation in March 1955, it set about getting its own affiliated unions to separately collect demands from their members. Apart from that, Sactu also went out to canvas the affiliates of Tucsa [Trade Union Council of South Africa], and uncommitted unions as well. We held mass meetings directly in

the factories.

Nair: As we did with our Stay-at-homes, we ignored the leadership of Tucsa wholly, knowing that the leadership would not support *any* political struggles whatsoever, let alone any struggle of Congress. So appeals were made directly to the workers.

Q: How did you get into the factories?

Nair: Now, first of all we distributed leaflets to the factories, to explain to the workers as to what the Congress of the People was all about. This was done not only in Sactu factories but in all factories, even factories affiliated to Tucsa.

Thereafter we got permission of the contacts that we had in the various Tucsa factories, to enter the factories, to have group discussions with the workers, in little groups of about 30, 40 workers. So we then succeeded, in very many many instances, in entering the cloakrooms of these factories, illegally, without management knowing, but with the workers actually collaborating.

This was done mainly in Tucsa unions. For instance, we had a very strong Congress-committed committee functioning in the garment industry. We had a similar committee functioning in the leather industry — all affiliates of Tucsa!

Q: Of the Tucsa unions?

Nair: Of the Tucsa unions.

Q: How did you do that? How did you get permission to do that?

Nair: The workers were encouraged to submit *any* demand which they thought was important — even if it were repeated by other workers.

Q: Billy, what sort of demands did you collect from the workers?

Nair: Among the demands that were frequently made was the call for a fully paid 40-hour week. You will find that demand in the Freedom Charter today. Another important demand that found its way into the Freedom Charter was that all who work should be free to form trade unions. That question was vital at the time for African workers — and, I should add, it still is.

Although many trade unions have recognition today, it does not follow that trade unions are free. Freedom to form trade unions means more than mere trade union recognition in law. Our progressive trade unions are still constantly harassed.

Q: How were the actual demands collected?

Nair: That's an important question. Because of the difficulty of getting into factories we had to rely often on the workers themselves collecting demands within their factories. Often we got a set of collective demands coming from the factory. We found the workers often acting as a collective because they were there in the factory situation under one roof.

Q: What percentage of Durban workers do you think you got across to in the factories?

Nair: Ja, well, I wouldn't say all the factories sent delegates.

Q: But did you get through to them all?

Nair: Ja. Insofar as the canvassing was concerned we left...no...stone...unturned in getting to *all* factories.

Q: So you tried to get to all?

Nair: No! Not tried, in fact we *did*. Ja. All. Not just with a single leaflet, but with a *series* of leaflets, both at a Sactu level and at a Joint Congress level. ■

All in all the collection of demands also enabled Sactu to push forward one of its major aims —

organising unorganised workers. This is what one Port Elizabeth Sactu organiser said:

Organiser: The campaign helped us a lot. The workers would bring their demands to the Sactu offices after work. We worked till late and they would come in with their papers from different industries. The real organising of workers was boosted by the Freedom Charter campaign. You see, they had something to keep them together to discuss common problems. Some of their problems were those of higher wages, better working conditions, and then with the set up in South Africa this can only be solved by having a union. We explained that workers must unite, have a union to represent them. So this gave us a chance to organise workers.

Sactu national official, Lesley Mesina, presenting the clause "There shall be work and security" at the Congress of the People. Next to him is Father Trevor Huddleston.

11. "I can do something in the organiser side"

'MaNyembe' tells how she got involved during the Defiance Campaign and became a key Natal organiser for the Congress of the People.

Another activist who played an outstanding role in Durban in the Congress of the People campaign was Dorothy Nyembe, 'MaNyembe', as she is known. She was born in northern Natal in 1932. In her childhood, her family were small-scale peasants forced to become labour tenants on a white farm. MaNyembe has done 18 long years in prison. Her second term, a 15 year stretch, she has only just completed.

Q: MaNyembe, what brought you into the struggle?
Nyembe: I came to Durban. I was 17 years old. I was working in a surgery by the beach, Marine Parade. I was cleaning and taking the names of those who were sick, to write on the cards. At that time I heard there was a meeting at the place which was called Red Square.
Q: Where is Red Square today?
Nyembe: Today it is a big building, a parking garage. So I went there. Then I listen. What these people talking about? They are telling about our oppression, and those words spoke also about my *own* life.

In my childhood my father was a small farmer at a Lutheran missionary station. After that we had to move to the white farms. My father was an attendant, a worker for this white farmer.

One day that farmer, he came to my father. He said my father must come cut off all his oxen. He must sell our cattles. He must sell to reduce his stock. I remember my father. He was looking like he was sick. The whole month. He couldn't talk. Just looking. Looking. And after that the stock was reduced.

I was wondering inside, what man is this my father is afraid of? Why he couldn't take a *sjambok* and hit that man who comes here to say he must reduce his stock? Everybody, they lower their heads when this farmer passed. But I looked at that farmer. He's got two feet, no? Two hands only. Why they are afraid of him? Now I'm growing this hatred against these people.

So that first political meeting I attended in Red Square reminded me of my own life. Soon after that I became a volunteer in the Defiance Campaign. When the men call upon those who can volunteer to go to jail for breaking the laws, I was the first to raise my hands. I will fight against these laws! ■

At that stage MaNyembe was a young woman, just 19 years old.

Nyembe: So they look at me. I said: "I will!"

When I went to the ANC offices Chief Luthuli said: "My child, these people don't believe you will do it. It's not easy." Luthuli said first I must prove myself by organising Cato Manor where I lived.

In no time I was getting 29 people as volunteers. I sent them down to the office. People started to listen to me after that! *They find that I can do something in the organiser side.* ■

Apart from organising, MaNyembe was involved in

Dorothy Nyembe ('MaNyembe'): When the men call upon those who can volunteer to go to jail for breaking the laws, I was the first to raise my hands. I will fight against these laws."

acts of defiance herself. Then, with the launch of the Congress of the People campaign in 1954, she was again active as an organiser.

Nyembe: We started in our branches (ANC and Women's League) in Cato Manor and Durban Central. We started to talk with the people about the Freedom Charter. In Cato Manor I was calling a meeting every Wednesday.

Q: How many people would come to these meetings?

Nyembe: Sometimes we found that in Cato Manor on Saturday you can get 5 000. In the week, by the daytime you got 300, sometimes 200.

Q: You were collecting demands for the Freedom Charter at these meetings?

Nyembe: Yes. The audience would raise their hands. We used to let members of the audience speak their views. We would write down the demands, all the demands. Also we went house to house.

Q: What happened if you went to a house? What would you say?

Nyembe: I was just getting to the house. I say: "Here I am. I come from the ANC office. I am the voice of Chief Luthuli, he say that and that and that and that and that and that…."

Q: And what did the people say?

Nyembe: They say: "Ohhh!" [MaNyembe claps her hands.] "Chief Luthuli!" [She laughs.]

Chief Albert Luthuli was president of the ANC from 1952 till his death in 1967. When Dorothy Nyembe went to people's homes, she would say: "I am the voice of Chief Luthuli". This would open all doors.

12. "Straight away you're a comrade"

One of the outstanding features of the Congress of the People campaign was the way in which the collection of demands helped build non-racialism. This is one aspect to which A.S. Chetty kept returning.

A.S. Chetty was born and bred in Pietermaritzburg. Today he is an executive member of the Natal Indian Congress (NIC).

Chetty: I come from a middle class background. My father was a builder, my mother a housewife and Tamil school teacher. I got involved in NIC politics soon after school. We used to do a lot of pamphleteering, and a lot of painting of the walls and all that. Those days we painted "Resist this", "Resist that"...whatever the campaign was, "Support the Potato Boycott", "Support the Cigarette Boycott".

The leader of the NIC here was Dr M. Motala at that time. NIC was becoming quite a strong unit in Pietermaritzburg. But what helped us very much was the ANC.

During the Congress of the People campaign we had a very strong branch of the ANC here under the leadership of Archie Gumede. Harry Gwala was also very, very important. The ANC was a well-knit body, which helped the NIC here. We formed a strong alliance and worked together on the question of the campaign.

African people were very co-operative with Indian volunteers, in both the urban and rural areas. When we Indians go into an African area there was *no* question, you know, that the guy's going to assault you. The moment you give them the sign, you're a comrade. You say: *"Afrika!"* and they return it: *"Mayibuye!"* Straight away you're a comrade. Open, come into the house and talk. ■

But acceptance of the non-racial spirit was sometimes more difficult to foster in the Indian areas.

Chetty: It took a hell of a time to break the old pattern. It was mainly by our *action* at the time, mainly in 'Maritzburg, where we can actually physically portray to people that we can jointly together do things. Because this idea of association with Africans was a hell of a bogey created by the oppressors at that time. *Swartgevaar* was a real bogey, and it made our task very difficult.

Despite these problems in the Indian areas, the NIC had already made a considerable impact. As A.S. Chetty discovered in house-to-house work in the Pietermaritzburg Indian community, Dr Motala of the NIC was, in particular, well-known and respected.

Chetty: The moment you mention Dr Motala's name, then straight away they know it's political. Then we explain the Congress of the People campaign, what it is all about: "Before we can form the Charter we need demands. These are some of the demands the people are calling for. Would you like to add to these demands? Have you got any grievances?" In the main, at the time, it was housing, housing, housing.

At one or two homes you used to get these fellows arguing politically, you know! "Oh, you fellows are wasting your time", "you can achieve nothing in this country", "we are quite happy with what the government is doing for us", that kind of talk.

There was one fellow, I remember, I went on explaining about the importance of the Congress of the People and the Charter, about *everything* that's connected with liberation in this country. (You know, in your enthusiasm as a youth you could do that.) I went ahead, I went ahead, and then in the end he said: "Ay, man, how much donation you want?"

I said: "I'm not asking for donations, man. I'm explaining to you what the Freedom Charter is."

He said: "Ay, you talking so long. Here you are man, take five shillings and go!"

Q: But what would you do if you got reactionary demands? Write them down?

Chetty: Ja. We would write them down. We would write the difficult ones down. At our group assessment afterwards we would ask: "Now how do we tackle this?" We would work out the best plan. Then the guy who had been to the particular house in the first place will take two others and go back there. They'd sit down with the person and start talking.

The moment we went the second time the person would usually say: "Look, no man, I'm sorry. I hope I didn't hurt your feelings. But this is my view, if you can tell me if I'm correct or not." Ja. It was a tiring task.

Q: Who do you remember playing a leading role in Pietermaritzburg during the campaign?

Chetty: Archie Gumede, Dr Motala, Harry Gwala, William Khanyile of Sactu (he was killed in the Matola raid), Moses Mabhida, the late S.P. Mungle, the late Dr Omar…S.P. Mungle was such a popular guy. He had his whole life dedicated to the movement. Every Saturday afternoon he used to go around selling the *New Age*. The moment he walks into the Indian village down at the bottom end of town the kids would gather around him: "Ja, Communist Party uncle, come this way, come this way."

We all used to sell the *New Age* at that time at a tickey, then five pence a copy. That was a ritual. Saturday afternoons it was part of our programme. The *New Age* played a very important role in propagating the Congress of the People campaign. ■

The volunteers from Pietermaritzburg did not confine themselves to the town and its vicinity.
Chetty: We didn't plan our organisational programme with a view to just contacting people in the urban areas. We planned it in such a way that we make sure we go out to the rural areas. Both ANC and NIC together went along to practically every house in the various districts of Pietermaritzburg and its surroundings. Districts such as Willowfontein, Edendale, Plessieslaer, Cato Ridge, Elandskop. Then Richmond, as far as Greytown, Wartburg, in the south, Harding, Estcourt, Lions River, all the rural areas, Kranskop, Howick. There was quite a few, man — right up to Ixopo.

We had activists at the time who were prepared to do this, you know, trudge along on foot in all the rural areas.

Q: Could you describe a typical house visit in the rural areas?
Chetty: We had to very respectfully abide by some customs and regulations. You can't just walk into an African house. It's a hut type house, right. You tap at the door and stand outside. Then our African comrade, whoever it is, Moses [Mabhida] or

A.S. Chetty, executive member of the Natal Indian Congress: "We had activists at the time who were prepared to do this, you know, trudge along on foot in all the rural areas."

whoever it is, says: "Ja, sawubona."

The woman of the house will first come over and say: "Sawubona." Then she won't talk to you, she'll go inside.

Then the man comes up. "Right, now what you come for?"

And Moses or Archie would say: "We are from the ANC." (The rural people don't know the NIC.)

"Au, sawubona. Okay, okay, come and sit down, sit on the verandah, and tell us your business."

We tell them the business in English and you've got an interpreter, or the African comrade just explains straight away in Zulu. When we tell the guy the business he automatically gets more people to come in. The guys used even to pass the beer can around, to you.

Now we start explaining why we are there. Right. They listen and listen and ask questions.

Q: Does the wife take part in this?

Chetty: No, the wife doesn't. In African rural areas women generally didn't take part. The man was asking us the questions. The women just kept quiet. That was a very strong tradition.

Q: Did you take women comrades with you into these areas?

Chetty: No. In the urban areas we had women volunteers assisting. But I tell you we had a very, very small contingent of women at that time. Ja. No, we didn't have very many women.

Q: How were the demands collected?

Chetty: We used to use the forms that were sent to us from Johannesburg. Then we used to print our own over and above that. But people in the rural areas actually used to write out their demands on scraps of paper, on brown paper. A lot of people used to send in the demands themselves.

Sometimes demands weren't collected immediately. People would think about it after our house to house visits. It was a tiring organisational task. You had to go to the people not on one occasion, but two or three occasions sometimes, you see. To collect their demands.

Q: Did you have any contact with chiefs?

Chetty: We didn't contact very many chiefs, but there were some sympathetic chiefs in Edendale. Chief Mini was one fellow who was very sympathetic. He played a very important role in this whole thing. He was to a large extent responsible for calling up quite a few meetings in his area. I think he's still alive today, but he's been deposed as chief.

There were also some chiefs in the Ladysmith area who were very sympathetic. They used to get their people together for us to come and speak to them. We used to go out very, very early on a Sunday, before the people go to church. Then the chief would arrange for us to speak to them straight after the church service. ■

Another volunteer who was collecting demands in the rural areas of Natal was Dorothy Nyembe. She remembers going to northern Natal.

Q: What places in northern Natal?

Nyembe: Ladysmith, Vryheid and Hlobane — the place of my childhood. Pietermaritzburg area, Utrecht, round Nqutu, down to Babanango. I remember I went to Ingwavuma three times. We go down to Newcastle. Then we came this side. We go to Ixopo, until Umzimkulu.

Q: What sort of demands came from the rural areas?

Nyembe: I remember, the people outside there they wanted that they must get enough space.

Q: Enough land for themselves?
Nyembe: Yes. Even now they still want more land, more cattles.

The struggle for land remains a crucial element of the democratic struggle.

13. "He comes to his sober senses"

Sometimes volunteers would encounter people who were scared to express their views or voiced reactionary demands. Here volunteers recall some of the problems encountered in the Johannesburg area.

We meet Aaron Mahlangu at the General and Allied Workers Union (Gawu) offices in Chancellor House, downtown Johannesburg. Outside on the pavements things are shifting, knots of lunch-time workers and the smell of deep fries from the quick take-away joints. This is downtown Jo'burg.

As we drive along these streets Mahlangu points out landmarks. "That over there, see, it's the old Mayibuye School." With his ongoing commentary we never do get to find out what, precisely, the Mayibuye School was.

Aaron Mahlangu is a tall man, a Sactu stalwart in his time, and one of the final thirty in the notorious Treason Trial. An organiser to his fingertips, it is hard to get Mahlangu to talk specifically about the Congress of the People campaign. He displays, rather, a lively interest in present-day campaigns. This ongoing interest has earned Mahlangu the fruits of a lifetime in the struggle — in short, he is flat broke. He seldoms knows where tomorrow's bus fare is coming from.

Never mind, the struggle continues. "Ja, I'm too good at organising, man. All my life the bosses have been dismissing me from jobs."

Q: Could we speak a little about the Congress of the People campaign?

Mahlangu: Sure. You're calling the tune. From now on I'll only talk about the Congress of the People campaign! ■

Mahlangu's main activity in collecting demands was on the workers' front.

Mahlangu: I was a *volontiya*. We were collecting demands in a manner which we afterwards called the M-plan. From each and every factory we had to collect. We used to establish factory contacts. You call these contacts, regionally and provincially.

During lunch hours they discussed this [the Congress of the People] and after their discussion they say: "Now let's sit down and put our demands".

Q: Were the demands all as expected?

Mahlangu: Some not. We didn't really expect that workers in factories would say that courts of law should be as impartial as ever. Many of that sort. Each one comes with opinion. ■

Did the collecting of demands in the Transvaal urban areas always go smoothly? We wanted to hear from old volunteers about the problems they encountered.

Martin Ramokgadi lives in Alexandra. He cuts a tall, impressive figure. At 74 he remains clear and coherent. He is also a man of few words. He answers each question precisely, and then stops.

Ramokgadi, like so many others we interviewed, has served long periods in jail. He has done two long sentences, lasting altogether nearly two decades. We asked Ramokgadi if people were ever difficult during the collection of demands.

Ramokgadi: Sometimes you find a man who doesn't understand politics at all. He says: "Look here, I'm not a politician. I don't want to be asked."

Aaron Mahlangu, a former Sactu leader and Treason Trialist: "From each and every factory we had to collect demands."

Q: So what did you say then?
Ramokgadi: So you say to him: "Are you happy staying in this small room, isolated from people who got the means? Do you like passes? Are you happy that your children get inferior education?"
Q: Did that work?
Ramokgadi: I mean, then surely he comes out and says: "No, I'm not."
Q: And then?
Ramokgadi: Then you ask him more questions which really worry him. "Are you happy this?" He says: "No." "Are you happy that?" "No."

And so the reactionary approach goes away. *He comes to his sober senses.* He starts to remember. ∎

Working in Fordsburg, Amin Cajee remembers people being generally cooperative, but a few also gave problems.

Cajee: When I worked with Prema's father [Roy Naidoo], a couple of people refused to answer. One or two people, I remember, *hardly* you can speak to them. This one house, they've got Gandhi's photo in there. The chap says: "No, we don't want to involve ourselves in politics."

So Prema's father Roy — we called him Roy — say: "Take this photo off! What the hell is the matter with you? Why do you want to keep his photo when you talk like that?"

So that way Roy used to pound them down, hey! He got them to give demands. Roy was Tamil-speaking, but he was speaking Gujerati very fluently to that chap! ∎

The Freedom Charter campaign was combined with other campaigns of the time. In the Transvaal the apartheid government was in the process of demolishing Sophiatown.

Q: How was the Sophiatown anti-removal campaign linked to the Congress of the People campaign?
Esakjee: Look, that time there was a big uproar about the removal of Sophiatown. These people being under threat of being removed made more demands. First of all the demand: "We don't want to be removed". We combined both campaigns. ∎

David Mahopa was living in Sophiatown at that time. He was one of the many thousands soon to be forcibly moved out. He remembers combining collecting demands for the Congress of the People with the Sophiatown anti-removal campaign and the campaign against Bantu education.

Mahopa: We telling them that under the Charter everyone will have a place where he will build a house. Bantu Education will be abolished. We shall have a general education. ∎

When he speaks of his own misfortunes Mahopa smiles and shrugs his shoulders, he makes light of his own sufferings. When he describes how his own home was bulldozed away he makes it sound like a comic affair. But his tone and expressions change completely when his own story is not the central point. He has nothing but anger when he speaks of the people's suffering and a burning sense of duty in the struggle to remove oppression.

Mahopa: In Sophiatown, we were organising by street. We were organising people one street, one street, one street and then telling them about the Congress of the People and collecting demands. We organise street by street. We have leaders in each street. They first go to each house. After that they call a meeting in a certain house in a street. They get

David Mahopa: "In Sophiatown, we were organising by street. We were organising people one street, one street, one street."

demands at these meetings.

Q: Was there any hostility?

Mahopa: At first there was some hostility. Some people would say: "You are saying these things all the time. You can't do nothing [laughter]. You can't do nothing" [laughter].

We said: "No. We must struggle. We must fight. We must show them…" ■

How fully did women participate in the formulation of demands? The picture we got varied from one Transvaal area to the next.

Ramokgadi: Our aim was to get the views of everybody. But in some families you find the man dominating. Where the man says: "No, what I say is final", then we don't interfere. That is a domestic matter. You don't go further. But that was a very small percentage.

Really, women took part. We used to tell the people that we would like the women and children over twenty to say something.

Nanabhai: I went mostly round the Gujerati community. Most of the volunteers would invite the women to participate. But the women would be shy, 'specially the older generation.

Vandeyar: I think one must look at the make-up of our communities. Traditionally, amongst the Indian people, the womenfolk usually took the backseat. It was the men of the house who would be the spokesperson for the family. In a few cases only were things different, maybe a daughter that has been going to university or college, then you got the womenfolk speaking out.

But in other areas, the coloured areas for instance, we found the women were mostly the dominant figures.

Q: In which coloured areas did you collect demands?

Vandeyar: Coronationville, Albertsville, Noordegesig. You found that the coloured women, because many of them were factory workers, would be able to come out with a lot of grievances about houses and wages.

In the African townships (I went to quite a number of places like Alexandra township, Sophiatown, Newclare), here again you would find the men were dominant. Now there I think it was the language barrier. The men could speak English more easily.

14. "People not having land of their own"

Volunteers from Johannesburg travelled great distances to reach the smaller towns and rural districts of the province.

For Amin Cajee travelling into the rural districts to collect demands was a case of going back to his roots. Cajee, a veteran executive member of the Transvaal Indian Congress, was born in Schweizer-Reinecke. The same far Western Transvaal town was the birthplace, as Cajee proudly informs us, of one of the Rivonia trialists currently serving a life sentence in prison.

Cajee: Kathy [Ahmed Kathrada] and I are home-boys, we both from Schweizer. ■

Amin Cajee himself has had his taste of jails. In 1947 he travelled down to Durban, to participate in the Passive Resistance campaign. He was arrested and sentenced to 30 days.

Cajee: I was sent to Durban Central to break stones. You sit on one stone and put another big stone in front of you. They give you a two-and-a-half pound hammer, and then you break the stone into little pebbles. They used the pebbles on the station platforms. I believe the Railways used to pay the Prisons two shillings per prisoner per day — hmm! — for the stones.

As we finish off for the day, they used to have this business of *tausa*. You know, you strip yourself completely. You show your mouth first, open wide. Then you jump in the air, show your backside for the *poyisa* [police] who is standing there. To make sure you are not smuggling anything back to the cells.

After a few days we refused to do this. We went on a hunger strike, five of us.... ■

And Cajee's story continues.

During the Defiance Campaign he travelled back to his birthplace in the Western Transvaal.

Cajee: We went to Schweizer-Reinecke and to Vryburg. The late Babla Saloojee [who died in detention], myself, and Mosey Moolla. At Vryburg we went to the African location there. A municipal

Amin Cajee has been active since the time of the Passive Resistance campaign. During the Congress of the People campaign he went out to the rural areas with people like Babla Saloojee, who died in detention in 1964.

cop tells us: "Go to such and such a place, don't go there, there that a bladdy policeman." A municipal cop tells us!

In no time, in less than an hour, we got 40 volunteers. That very night they defied. There, nine o'clock they ring the bell, and Africans got to go out of the town for the curfew. They defied that. ∎

It was on the basis of these volunteer groups, formed in the Defiance Campaign, that door-to-door collecting of demands was carried out for the Congress of the People campaign in the Western Transvaal.

Q: Were the demands from the Western Transvaal different from the demands of the people in the urban areas?

Cajee: They were about the same, you know. Only a little bit different. That cattle dipping issue came up in the reserves. And then wages, wages were very little. Sometimes you get ten shillings a week wages there in places like Schweizer and Vryburg. ∎

Amin Cajee was also involved in travelling to the Eastern Transvaal.

Cajee: Mostly it was setting up teams, committees, in all the African townships. I was travelling around with an ANC comrade, MacDonald Maseko. We'd hold a meeting, and then give them instructions what to do to get more people. ∎

The task of Cajee and Maseko was not, therefore, to collect demands as such, but to assist the development of local teams of volunteers to carry out this work.

Cajee: We went to all these places like Belfast, Breyten, Carolina, Bethal, then we came down to Ermelo, and then we land in jail there. Hmmm, mmmh.

We had a contact in Breyten. He stood there by the roadside. He guided us into the township. We distributed Congress of the People leaflets all over.

Then when we got to Ermelo the cops got us and laid charges, that we tried to incite. They say we must pay a fine of admission of guilt.

Next day we appeared in court for a formal remand. In the court there was all these chiefs from Swaziland.

Q: What did the Swazi chiefs have to do with it?

Cajee: They had heard of our arrest from their followers in the Eastern Transvaal townships. They were very good, you know, those chiefs. They were very big supporters of the ANC.

They said that, no, even if we get jail, we must fight the case. We mustn't pay the fine and give in like that.

Then Dr Yusuf Dadoo came by taxi to ask us what we going to do: "To fight it!" we say. He agreed.

We won the case. I wouldn't have minded if we'd got one year or two years or six months. Ah, it would have been alright man. Hey, all the chiefs were delighted. Politically it was a good thing. ∎

Another Jo'burg volunteer who remembers going out into the rural areas is David Mahopa.

Mahopa: I was one of the volunteers. We went out by cars to Rustenburg, Platinum Mine, Phokeng, to Brits, to that village, Makau. We went to Pietersburg by train to organise. I talked to chiefs. Then to Pietersburg location. I held a meeting with the advisory boards of Pietersburg and Potgietersrust. I went to Warmbaths and Hammanskraal.

The advisory boards and chiefs cooperated with me for meetings. Some made constructive suggestions. They say: "No, this is a good thing." This is what they were *telling* me. I don't know what they were saying after I went away! ■

Solly Esakjee of Fordsburg was also collecting demands in the Transvaal rural areas.

Q: What demands came from the rural areas?
Esakjee: Against pass laws — abolition of pass laws, against Bantu education, and prison labour.
Q: Did you get demands you expected?
Esakjee: Look, a demand like the repeal of pass laws, that we expected. But there were a lot of other demands — *people not having land of their own*, was a very big demand in the rural areas.

Suliman Esakjee, a Treason Trialist, collected demands under difficult circumstances in such rural areas as Middelburg, Bethal and Ermelo.

Q: So you hadn't expected land hunger to be such a problem?

Esakjee: No. What we expected the big issue to be was the pass laws. But demands such as land for farm labourers...we didn't expect so much.

Q: Did you have much harassment from the farmers?

Esakjee: No. We really moved about at night [laughter]. At some places we did have harassment. At some place, I can't remember, the farmer wanted to shoot us and we had to get away.

Q: In what rural areas did you go collecting demands?

Esakjee: Personally, I went up to Middleburg, Bethal, Ermelo. A chap that I must mention here is Babla Saloojee, he did a lot of work himself. Babla, Gert Sibande and myself. We used to go out on Friday night and come back Monday morning. And in these rural areas people were got together, right out on the farms. Mainly Africans, and Gert would explain to them what the Congress of the People was, and we collected demands. And I'm just talking now of one group that went out, but there were many of these groups that went out.

Q: Did you go to the white-owned farms?

Esakjee: Yes. The work was mostly done on weekends, and we get together on the farm, in their mud houses.

In our group I remember Gert had a lot of contacts especially Ermelo way, Eastern Transvaal. There were no ANC branches as such.

Q: How many people would you get in such meetings?

Esakjee: It depends on that area. For instance, Bethal where Gert was, I remember, I think we had a meeting of 500 people because he was from that area. Then we went to a place, Jane Furse Hospital. Now there we met all the nurses at this hospital. And one nurse was elected as a delegate to come to the Congress of the People, and she was there.

So the demands that were collected during this period were genuine demands from the people.

Q: Who else do you remember going out to rural areas?

Esakjee: Lilian Ngoyi, James Radebe, Robert Resha, Stanley Lollan, he was a coloured.

Q: Did whites go to rural areas?

Esakjee: Yes, there was Ronny Press, the Levy Brothers, there was Percy Cohen — uh — Wolfie Kodesh. They went out to African areas.

Q: When you went to rural areas, did you go to Indian areas as well?

Esakjee: In the rural areas — in going to the Indians we made a special effort to go another time. Because the moment they saw an African, an Indian, and a white and a coloured it was looking for trouble, and the police would be there immediately. So, we try to make it, when we go to the Indian people, that it was only Indians that went, so there was no suspicion from the police. The importance of this campaign as I saw it was bringing the Congress of the People to the rural areas.

Q: Had the Defiance Campaign not had as much impact on rural areas?

Esakjee: I doubt it. In many parts, the Congress of the People campaign was the first time they heard of the alliance between Indians, whites and Africans.

BULLETIN OF THE TVL. PROVINCIAL COMMITTEE OF THE CONGRESS OF THE PEOPLE

FORWARD TO FREEDOM

OUR STICKERS
Have you seen them about? Like those at the bottom of the page. There are plenty more to be put up, so get some from your Volunteer-in-Chief immediately. VOLUNTEERS, make it your business to see that every member of your Branch takes some, and that they don't only stick to the lining of peoples' pockets!

March 1st, 1955.
NO. 2

MOBILISE and ORGANISE

The time is already past that the world should know what a sham democracy is in our country and how desperate are the needs of our people.

The time is already past that our people should have won their freedom.

The situation cries out for something to be done. So let us all, members of the four Congresses and their allies, put our shoulders to the wheel of the Congress of the People and make it an overwhelming success.

We must work fast and furiously - the date set for holding the Congress of the People is not later than June of this year. We have just 4 months.

WHAT IS TO BE DONE?

(1.) Is there a Volunteer group functioning in your area? If not, get to it.

(2) Has everybody in your area read a copy of the "Call", a leaflet explaining the campaign? Make it your business to see that they have.

(3) Demands to be incorporated in the Freedom Charter, which will be drawn up by the Congress of the People, are now pouring in. Are demands from your area included? You had better check up.

(4) A set of lecture notes are available which are entitled "The World We Live In". It is your duty to get hold of a copy and study it. Also, assist others to know its contents. If you would like a speaker to address a group on the subject, make your request to the Transvaal Provincial Committee and he or she will be right along.

An idea has been given of what is required of us. On with the good work. Organise and mobilise the people here and now!
FORWARD TO A VITAL AND MIGHTY CONGRESS OF THE PEOPLE!

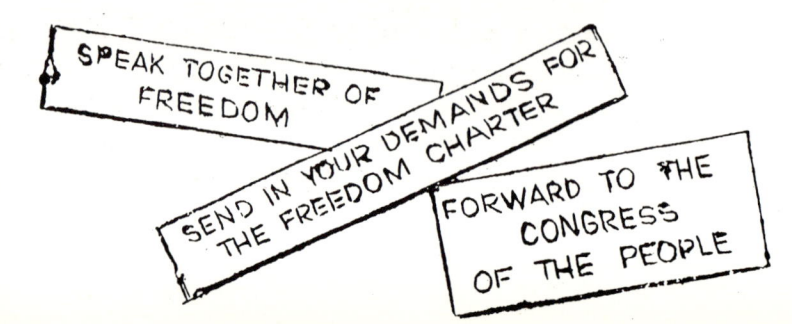

SPEAK TOGETHER OF FREEDOM

SEND IN YOUR DEMANDS FOR THE FREEDOM CHARTER

FORWARD TO THE CONGRESS OF THE PEOPLE

This cyclostyled bulletin, issued in the Transvaal, was one of the ways used to give impetus to the Congress of the People campaign.

15. Document: "Call to the Congress of the People"

During the collection of demands, thousands of copies of this leaflet were issued urging people to "Speak of Freedom".

WE CALL THE PEOPLE OF SOUTH AFRICA BLACK AND WHITE — LET US SPEAK TOGETHER OF FREEDOM!

WE CALL THE FARMERS OF THE RESERVES AND TRUST LANDS.
Let us speak of the wide land, and the narrow strips on which we toil.
Let us speak of brothers without land, and of children without schooling.
Let us speak of taxes and of cattle, and of famine.
LET US SPEAK OF FREEDOM.

WE CALL THE MINERS OF COAL, GOLD AND DIAMONDS.
Let us speak of the dark shafts, and the cold compounds far from our families.
Let us speak of heavy labour and long hours, and of men sent home to die.
Let us speak of rich masters and poor wages.
LET US SPEAK OF FREEDOM.

WE CALL THE WORKERS OF FARMS AND FORESTS.
Let us speak of the rich foods we grow, and the laws that keep us poor.
Let us speak of harsh treatment and of children and women forced to work.
Let us speak of private prisons, and beatings and of passes.
LET US SPEAK OF FREEDOM.

WE CALL THE WORKERS OF FACTORIES AND SHOPS.
Let us speak of the good things we make, and the bad conditions of our work.
Let us speak of the many passes and the few jobs.
Let us speak of foremen and of transport and of trade unions; of holidays and of houses.
LET US SPEAK OF FREEDOM.

WE CALL THE TEACHERS, STUDENTS AND THE PREACHERS.
Let us speak of the light that comes with learning, and the ways we are kept in darkness.
Let us speak of great services we can render, and of the narrow ways that are open to us.
Let us speak of laws, and government, and rights.
LET US SPEAK OF FREEDOM.

WE CALL THE HOUSEWIVES AND THE MOTHERS.
Let us speak of the fine children we bear, and of their stunted lives.
Let us speak of the many illnesses and deaths, and of the few clinics and schools.
Let us speak of high prices and of shanty towns.
LET US SPEAK OF FREEDOM.

LET US SPEAK TOGETHER

ALL OF US TOGETHER — African and European, Indian and Coloured. Voter and voteless. Privileged and rightless. The happy and the homeless. All the people of South Africa; of the towns and of the countryside.
LET US SPEAK TOGETHER OF FREEDOM. And of the happiness that can come to men and women if they live in a land that is free.
LET US SPEAK TOGETHER OF FREEDOM. And of how to get it for ourselves, and for our children.
LET THE VOICE OF ALL THE PEOPLE BE HEARD. AND LET THE

DEMANDS OF ALL THE PEOPLE FOR THE THINGS THAT WILL MAKE US FREE BE RECORDED. LET THE DEMANDS BE GATHERED TOGETHER IN A GREAT **CHARTER OF FREEDOM.**

WE CALL ON ALL GOOD MEN AND TRUE, to speak now of freedom, and to write their own demands into the Charter of Freedom.
WE CALL ALL WHO LOVE LIBERTY to pledge their lives from here on to win the Freedoms set out in the Charter.
WE CALL ALL THE PEOPLE OF SOUTH AFRICA TO PREPARE FOR:
THE CONGRESS OF THE PEOPLE — Where representatives of the people, everywhere in the land, will meet together in a great assembly, to discuss and adopt the Charter of Freedom.
Let us organise together for the Congress of the People.
Let us speak together of Freedom.
Let us work together for the Freedom Charter.
LET US GO FORWARD TOGETHER TO FREEDOM!

This Call to the **CONGRESS of the PEOPLE** is addressed to all South Africans, European and Non-European.

It is made by four bodies, speaking for the four sections of the people of South Africa: — by the African National Congress, the South African Indian Congress, the Congress of Democrats, and the South African Coloured People's Organisation.

It calls you all to prepare to send your chosen spokesman to:

THE CONGRESS OF THE PEOPLE,
a meeting of elected representatives of all races, coming together from every town and village, every farm and factory, every mine and kraal, every street and suburb, in the whole land. Here all will speak together of the things their people need to make them free. They will speak together freely, as equals.

They will speak together of changes that must be made in our lives, our laws, our customs and our outlooks. They will speak together of freedom. And they will write their demands into

THE FREEDOM CHARTER.
This Charter will express all the demands of all the people for the good life that they seek for themselves and their children. The Freedom Charter will be our guide to those "singing tomorrows" when all South Africans will live and work together, without racial bitterness and fear of misery, in peace and harmony.

THIS IS A CALL for an awakening of all men and women, to campaign together in the greatest movement of all our history. Our call is to you — the People of South Africa. We invite all Union-wide Organisations to join as sponsors of the CONGRESS OF THE PEOPLE, and to take part in its direction. Those who are not afraid to hear the voice of the people will join us. We will welcome them, and work together with them as equals.

We invite all local and provincial societies, clubs, churches, trade unions, sporting bodies and other organisations to join as partners in the CONGRESS OF THE PEOPLE Committee, and to share the work. Those who are not afraid to speak of freedom will join us. We will welcome them, and work together with them as equals.

We invite all South African men and women of every race and creed to take part as organisers of the CONGRESS OF THE PEOPLE and awaken others to its message. Those who are prepared to work together for freedom and the Freedom Charter will join us. We will welcome them, and go forward together with them to freedom.

OUR CALL IS TO YOU!
- Give your time to spread the message of the CONGRESS OF THE PEOPLE.
- Become a Volunteer to organise for freedom.
- Tell your neighbours and workmates of the nation-wide elections that are

coming.
- Rouse the people to discuss what they want of freedom.

LET US WORK TOGETHER FOR FREEDOM!

THE CONGRESS OF THE PEOPLE
will take place
- when all the people's demands for inclusion in the Freedom Charter have been gathered in;
- when the whole country has been awakened to speak of freedom, and the call for elections has been made;
- not later than June, 1955 — at a date and place still to be announced.

THE CONGRESS OF THE PEOPLE
will be organised
- by 50, 000 Volunteers, who will give their time to carrying through the campaign as directed;
- by a network of committees in every village, town and factory representing and uniting all sections and all races;
- by the National Action Council, composed of all national bodies that agree to act as sponsors.

DO THESE THREE THINGS — NOW!
ONE: SEND IN YOUR NAME AND ADDRESS TO A PROVINCIAL COMMITTEE OF THE CONGRESS OF THE PEOPLE, stating that you are interested and would like to assist.
TWO: FORM COMMITTEES to campaign for the Congress of the People.
THREE: GATHER GROUPS to send in their demands for the Freedom Charter.

●●●

DO NOT THROW THIS LEAFLET AWAY! PASS IT ON TO A FRIEND. DISCUSS IT WITH OTHERS. SEE THAT IT IS READ BY MANY PEOPLE.

Canvassing for the Congress of the People.

IV.
Electing delegates

16. The study class in Blouvlei

All over South Africa in meetings held in streets, factories and in the rural areas people elected their delegates to the Congress of the People.

In 1955 Amy Thornton was assisting a study class out at Blouvlei, Elsie's River.

Thornton: I went out there over a few years, every Monday night. Blouvlei was a squatter camp, one long sand dune, up and down. Wolfie Kodesh was the driver. We would drive along a tarred road with sand on each side. It would be absolutely pitch dark, featureless. But somehow Wolfie knew the area. Each time we would rendezvous at a different place. God knows how Wolfie recognised one spot from another. We'd stop, somebody would emerge from the night, and we'd go into the sand-dunes. Each Monday night we'd meet in a different *pondokkie*.

We'd sit around on handmade benches, with a candle in the middle. Dogs barking outside. It was mainly the men who participated; the wives would be nursing babies on the outskirts of the ring of light.

I remember reading Gorky's *Mother* for the first time in those years. I took it out to Blouvlei, and the comrades there couldn't believe that a book from such a faraway place could describe their own lives so accurately. The little huts, the furtive political discussions in the night, it was all there.

The core member of the study group was John Mtini. He was head of the local ANC branch, he was possibly a founder member of the ANC, and he was certainly one of the first Africans to join the

CPSA [Communist Party of South Africa]. He had been a contemporary of S.P. Bunting and of Johnny La Guma. Elijah Loza, who died in security police custody in 1977, was also a core member of the study group. So too was Bernard Huna.

In the study group we discussed the Congress of the People campaign. We read *The Call*. That was especially useful, it helped to structure people's demands. I remember the main complaint was passes, passes, always passes. Houses, jobs, those issues also always came up.

Over the Congress of the People campaign the different Congresses — African, Indian, coloured and the white COD [Congress of Democrats], really pulled together for the first time. In Cape Town we had a Joint Congress Committee [JCC]. I was secretary of the Cape Town JCC. The Indian Congress didn't really function in Cape Town, the Indian community was so tiny. But three of us, representing the other congresses, would go out to the country districts of the Western Cape. We'd usually have a contact person in the different *dorpies*. A small meeting would be convened. We'd speak about the Congress of the People, we'd leave leaflets behind, and the local comrades would then organise the collection of demands.

As the weekend for the Congress of the People came closer, people began electing delegates. They were real elections from small groupings scattered all over the country. I was elected as a delegate by the Congress of Democrats. When I told the study class at Blouvlei, they presented me with four shillings which they had collected among themselves. That was a lot of money in those days. You can imagine how honoured and moved I felt. ∎

Amy Thornton, Congress of Democrat activist: "There were real elections from small groupings scattered all over the country."

Amy Thornton was elected as a delegate by the Congress of Democrats. When we asked about how delegates were elected we got a different picture from different regions.

From the African townships in Cape Town, Christmas Tinto remembers delegates being official representatives of ANC branches.
Q: Did people in particular streets elect delegates?
Tinto: No. The delegates were not elected from those people you took grievances from.
Q: Couldn't they elect delegates?
Tinto: No. They give grievances. The area ANC, they call their meetings to read their demands of this area, they're put on a paper.
Q: In some places, non-ANC people could be delegates to the Congress of the People. Was that not possible in Langa?
Tinto: Well, a lot of people joined the ANC in that time. But there were not non-ANC members as delegates. ■

In other regions, it seems, delegates were not necessarily organisational representatives. Mahopa, active in Sophiatown at the time, was insistent on this point.
Mahopa: In Sophiatown people were elected as delegates from the streets.
Q: Did they have to be ANC members?
Mahopa: No, just people, never mind they are members or not.
Q: What type of people? Labourers, teachers or what?
Mahopa: Labourers, not teachers. Teachers were afraid to lose job. Even the ministers were afraid. They were supportive in a hidden way. ■

Dorothy Nyembe remembers a similar procedure being followed in Durban.
Q: When delegates were elected to Kliptown, how were they elected?
Nyembe: Oh! Heyi! I do not quite remember how many delegates.
Q: But how were they elected?
Nyembe: In meetings, you know. From Durban Central, Clairwood....
Q: Were people who were not Congress members sometimes elected as delegates?
Nyembe: When we went to the Congress of the People we did not go as members of the ANC. We were chosen by the people in the different areas to go there. ■

Also in the Durban region there were elections of workers' delegates at a factory level.
Nair: The most democratic methods were used. At the factory-floor level the workers met independently and elected the best people to send — three, four, five delegates, depending entirely on how much funds they were able to raise.
Q: Were workers actually able to collect such funds?
Nair: Oh, yes! Factory workers actually collected monies in the factories, we didn't spend union funds. We collected money among the workers to send workers directly from the factories to the Congress of the People. A similar thing was done on ANC and the Indian Congress levels. So the whole campaign for the collection of demands and the organisation of the Congress of the People was a massive campaign undertaken on a national scale.
Q: What happened if factories were unable to raise money for fares?

Nair: If, in a smaller factory, the workers were only able to muster part of the fare, Sactu made up for the balance, to send at least one delegate, provided the workers showed some keenness to collect funds themselves. Otherwise, in the main, workers collected their own funds. ■

The Congress of the People campaign itself lasted many long months. How did people manage to raise funds? This is what Solly Esakjee remembers.

Esakjee: A lot of money came in from the African people. I remember, before the Defiance Campaign, a stamp was issued, it was called the Million Shillings Stamp — something like that. And we used to go out selling these stamps. To raise funds. A lot of money came in from the working-class people.

Sactu tried to reach each and every factory. Here a Sactu organiser talks through a barbed wire fence.

17. Document: "Let us speak of freedom"

This leaflet outlines what preparations were needed for the Congress of the People. It covers every small detail to ensure its success.

What is the Congress of the People?

It is an assembly of delegates of all the people of South Africa, where they will speak of freedom and of how to get it: there they will adopt a Freedom Charter drawn up from all the views of all the people everywhere; of what they would do IF THEY COULD MAKE THE LAWS.

Who can send delegates to the Congress of the People?

Any group of men and women, no matter how many there are; they should live in the same street, block, village or town; or they should work together in the same factory, office, shop or farm.

How are delegates to be chosen?

By a vote of the people who come together in a meeting in a house, or in a hall in a village, where they can talk over and agree on what they want in the Freedom Charter, and what their spokesmen to the Congress of the People must say.

What are delegates to do?

They are to travel to Johannesburg, so as to arrive not later than 10 a.m. Saturday morning, June 25th, 1955. In Johannesburg, they are to report to the offices of the African National Congress, South African Indian Congress, South African Congress of Democrats, and the South African Coloured People's Organisation, whose addresses we insert at the end of this leaflet. They are to bring their own blankets. Where they have no friends to accommodate them for the night, accommodation will be provided.

Who is to pay for the food and travelling?

Those who elect the delegate must pay for his travelling, and give him five shillings for his food. If they are willing to speak of freedom they must be willing to collect money to help win it. Those who can, should collect food, mealies, potatoes, rice, for the delegate to take to the Congress of the People Delegates' Kitchen at the Congress.

What if money cannot be raised?

If every effort to raise the money fails, or if no one at your meeting can leave work to travel to Johannesburg, appoint a friend or any acquaintance who lives on the Witwatersrand to represent you. Write and tell him he is to attend and to speak for you, and tell him what you want him to say. Tell him to take your letter to one of the Congress offices, and to ask for a delegate's card.

What if you know no people on the Rand?

Then write to the Congress of the People Committee, P.O. Box 11045, Johannesburg. Tell them what kind of people you are, where you live, and where you work. Tell them what demands you have for the Freedom Charter. They will find a suitable person to represent you at the Congress of the People.

How do delegates get credential cards?

As soon as delegates have been elected, write to the Congress of the People Committee at the above address for a delegate's card, or ask your local Congress Branch Secretary for one. Fill it in carefully before giving it to the delegate.

What is to be done with demands for the Freedom Charter?

They should be written out in any language and be sent in now to the C.O.P. Committee, saying how many people were present when they were discussed, and which town or place of work they come from. Or, if time is too short, there is space for it to be written on the back of your delegate's card.

Who is to organise for all this?

You are: because you want freedom as much as anyone. Start by yourself; talk to your neighbour and your workmates. Organise a little meeting for them, then get them to do the same in other places. Write about it to your relations and friends especially in the countryside and the Reserves. BUT YOU DO IT!

When is this to be done?

NOW, RIGHT AWAY, TODAY! There is no time to lose. Delegates have to be elected; money for the fare to be collected! So do it now! The Congress of the People is on the 25th and 26th of June, 1955.

Now it is time for you to act!

WE CALL ALL THE CITIZENS OF SOUTH AFRICA!
Let our voices ring a call of liberty throughout the land!
It is time to speak of freedom.
Let us speak together of the things we need to make us free.
It is time to draw the Freedom Charter.
Let us plan together a life of liberty for all our people.
It is time for the CONGRESS OF THE PEOPLE.
Yes! Now it is time!

The Congress of the People

will be held in Kliptown, Johannesburg,
on June 25th and 26th, 1955.

There all the delegates of the people will assemble to speak of freedom.
There the **Freedom Charter** will be drawn up.

Now it is time for you to act!
We call YOU, citizens of South Africa!
It is time for YOU to say what you want written on the Freedom Charter.
It is for YOU to elect a delegate to speak for YOU at the CONGRESS OF THE PEOPLE!

It is time for YOU to work for your own freedom.
Read this leaflet carefully!
Do what it tells you to do!
Then pass it on to a friend.

> ONWARD to the CONGRESS of the PEOPLE!
> We the people of South Africa, both black and white, have an urgent task to perform...
> We are called upon to set down in writing those things which we would like to enjoy... until it is won.
> Yes, let us now set up the goal posts which are our objectives!
> Let us speak together of Freedom!
> Hereunder are some demands that have been sent in for inclusion in the....
>
> **FREEDOM CHARTER.**
>
> We Demand...
> - Votes for all South Africans, both black and white.
> - Higher wages and better working conditions.
> - Better homes and housing for all.
> - Land for the landless people.
> - Free and compulsory education for all children irrespective of race, colour or creed.
>
> What are your Demands?
> If you are a FARMER what are your demands?___
> If you are a worker on a farm, what are your demands?___
> If you are a WORKER IN A FACTORY, what are your demands?___
> If you are a TEACHER what are your Demands?___
> If you are a STUDENT, what are your demands?___
> If you are a PREACHER, what are your demands?___
> If you are a MOTHER, what are your demands?___
> If you are a BUS OWNER, what are your demands?___
> If you are a BUSINESSMAN, what are your demands?___

This form was used to assist in gathering demands. But the people themselves raised many other grievances and demands.

77

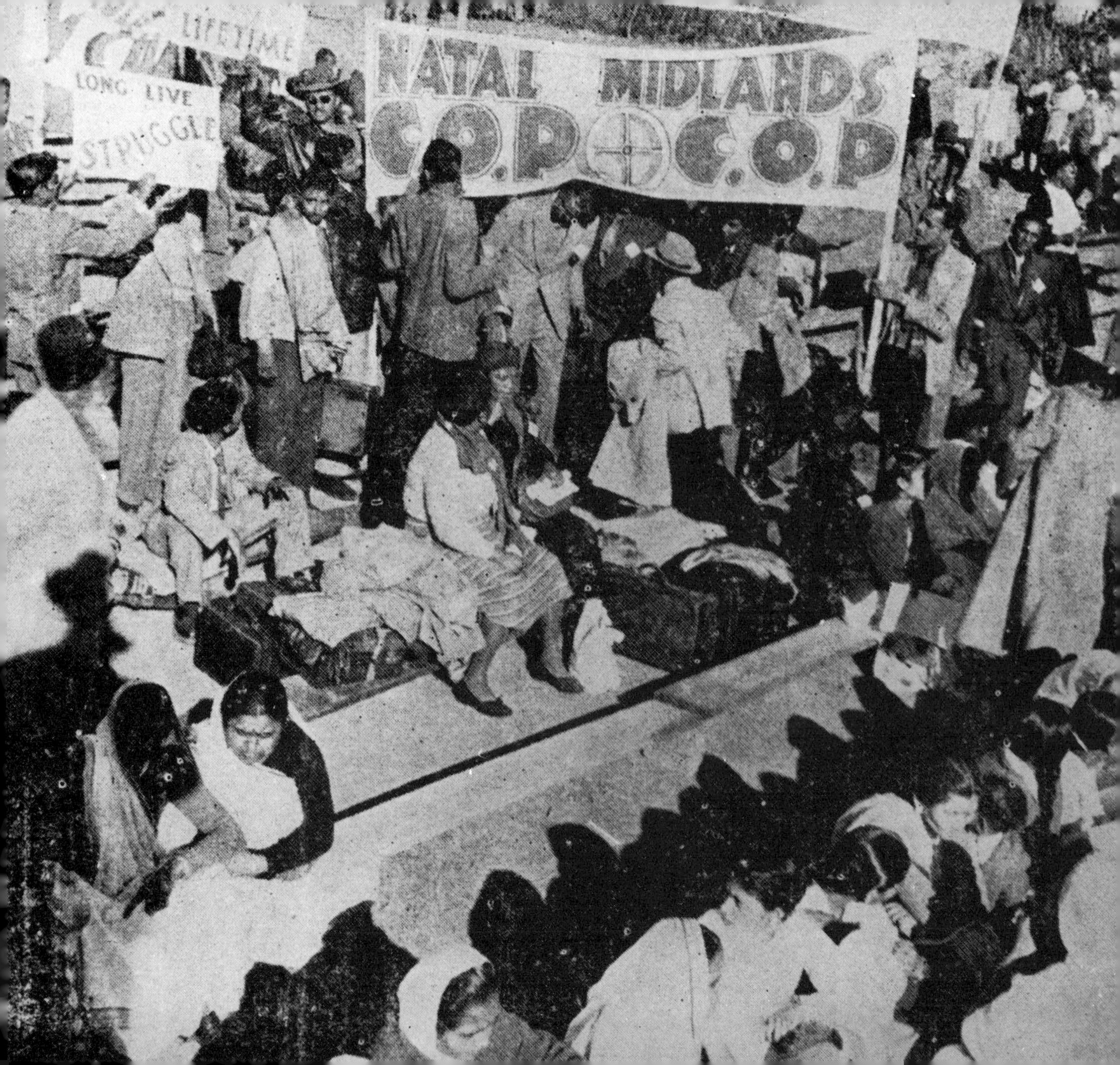
NATAL MIDLANDS
C.O.P. C.O.P.
LIFETIME
LONG LIVE
STRUGGLE

V. Travelling to Kliptown

◀ The Natal Midlands delegation arrived safely at the Congress of the People. They pretended they were a wedding party to get past a police roadblock.

18. Whistling the Internationale in Beaufort West

The apartheid government was determined to make it as difficult as possible to hold the Congress of the People. Many people were stopped on the way.

The weekend of the 25th and 26th of June 1955 was approaching. In the four corners of South Africa, after many months of campaigning, delegates had been elected. There had never been a campaign like it in the history of the South African struggle. According to Chief Albert Luthuli: "Nothing in the history of the liberatory movement in South Africa quite caught the popular imagination as this did, not even the Defiance Campaign. Even remote rural areas were aware of the significance of what was going on."[1]

However, the struggle to hold the Congress of the People was not yet over. Thousands of delegates had to be transported great distances to Kliptown. The apartheid government was determined to make life as difficult as possible for the delegates. On Friday 24th June the police were out in force.

The last time, in fact the only time Eileen van de Vindt left the Western Cape, was a June weekend in 1955. She was just 18 years old.

Eileen thinks back, as she looks out over the Cape Flats, with sand blowing around her tiny Lavender Hill council flat. She and her family were group area'd out here 13 years ago.

Van der Vindt: In 1955 I was involved with the

Coloured People's Congress. We were living in District Six with cockroaches as big as THIS, and rats the size of kittens, but it was home. Not like Lavender Hill. Agh, it was nice. When I think of District Six, I feel soft inside....Anyways, ja, I was going to this club in town. It had dancing classes and art classes. Albie Sachs used to be there, and George Peake, and a writer...man, a coloured chap...umm.

Q: La Guma?

Van der Vindt: *Jaa!* That's right *Alex* La Guma. What they were doing at this club was first to let us mix. Coloureds, whites, Africans, Indians together. It was still those days, you know, when that wasn't easy. A person used to feel could you, can you, must you, or what? They never spoke specifically about 'joining the ranks' or anything. It was for you to make up your own mind. Anyways, that's how I got involved, and that's how I came to be on the road to Kliptown! ■

The Western Cape delegates arranged to leave secretly on the Thursday before the Congress of the People.

Thornton: [looking back, laughs] Well it was *supposed* to be secret. Ben Turok was responsible for the arrangements. Two trucks were hired. There were secret pick-up points all along the way, Bellville, I remember, under the bridge outside Paarl, Worcester...there were 25 delegates in each truck.

I was up front in the cab with one of the drivers. It was my task to keep him awake. He wasn't an activist or anything. The moment we started he hauled out a bottle of brandy and began drinking.

Van der Vindt: We were going to Jo'burg, to Kliptown for the Congress of the People. It was in a lorry, about 30 of us from Cape Town, whites and coloureds and Africans. That was already a suspicion, I suppose.

At Beaufort West one of the comrades says: "Uh-uh. Look what's here." It was the police dressed up in private clothing. The comrade, a tall dark chap, whose name was...no, I can't remember, he said: "Whatever you say, say nothing."

"Where are you going?" the police asked. But nobody wanted to speak. We just said: "We are going to Joburg!" That was all.

Thornton: The police checked all the African comrades' passes. But there was nothing wrong there. Then they asked the drivers if they had permits to transport people. They didn't, so we were asked to accompany them to the police station. On the way Alf Wannenburgh, George Peake, Margaret Castle, and one or two others did a quick whip around for money, jumped off the trucks and ran for the station. That way they got to Kliptown. ■

In Beaufort West the police subpoena'd all the remaining delegates as witnesses in the case against the two drivers. The police were using every legal trick to prevent the delegates from getting to Kliptown. The lorries were impounded in the courtyard of the police station.

Thornton: I managed to phone Cape Town, Sam Kahn, or was it Brian Bunting in the *New Age* offices? I asked them to send some money to us. I hoped we might be able to use it to get people through to Kliptown. They promised that the money would be coming some time between 4.30

81

and 5.00 p.m. Alex La Guma and somebody else and I went down to the Cape Town end of Beaufort West. We waited and waited and waited. By 9.30 p.m. we decided to give up. We went back to the police station and we were let in through the charge office to the locked-up yard where our comrades were sleeping in the trucks.

Much later that night I heard knocking, somebody calling my name. It was Jack Tarshish, arrived from Cape Town with the money. He had just climbed up over the wall into the yard of the police station. He was highly agitated: "Didn't you hear me? I've been outside whistling the Internationale for the last half hour."

Van der Vindt: Next morning, Saturday, people came to smuggle us out to Jo'burg one by one. I got into the back of one car, hidden under blankets. We raced off, but too fast so the police noticed. They stopped the car, lifted the blankets and said to me: "Out!" Some got to Kliptown, but most of us were stuck in Beaufort West the whole weekend. We sang songs. Just working on the cops' nerves.

Thornton: The people in the African and coloured township heard about us. The remaining delegates were given a place to stay. You can imagine, the arrival of two truck loads of activists, black and white, was a sensational event for sleepy Beaufort West. It was a very, very depressed *dorpie* in those days. There was very litte employment. Our delegates were undeterred by the police harassment. They spent the weekend holding meetings in the township. They told the people about the Freedom Charter and Congress of the People. A Coloured People's Congress branch was established as a result of our weekend there!■

Not all the Western Cape delegates went on the trucks. One African delegate reported:

Delegate: Some of us got through in cars. I was in a car with a senior comrade, Albert Matinya, from Stellenbosch in those days, and I think Ben Turok, and let me see…It was quite a convoy of three or four cars. [silence] Ummm. We were stopped at about something to eight o'clock on the Friday morning, just before we entered Colesburg. It was a roadblock.

They searched the car. But we were waiting that we might be searched. A directive had gone out from the ANC; if you are on a mission make sure your passes are in order. In those days they must be signed every month. Also your taxes must be paid. It had happened the year before, I was at a volunteer's meeting at the Mowbray town hall. The SB's [Special Branch] raided the meeting, took all our names, checked our passes. A few weeks later I was arrested at work. I was locked up in Mowbray police station because of not paying poll tax. I should have paid as of 1944. And I had never paid until that time! [silence]

By 1955 my poll tax and pass was in order. So I got through the roadblock at Colesberg. But the senior comrade, Matinya, hadn't paid *his* poll tax. He was arrested there. We had to wait for him. We paid his fine and proceeded.

Friday night we got to Jo'burg. We went to the Congress offices. But there was a nine o'clock curfew in Johannesburg. We had to dodge. We from Cape Town were not used to the curfew.

The Wedding Party

A.S. Chetty was on one of the three lorries taking Natal Midlands delegates to Kliptown.

Chetty: We left Pietermaritzburg humorously. We took a lot of musical instruments. We sang songs on the way, as far as Heidelberg, our first stop. At Heidelberg you've got to produce your permits if you're an Indian, to get into the Transvaal. About five of us didn't have permits. Okay. We were marked fellows and we couldn't get permits. When we got to the border post we decided to work a scheme now. So we started making a hell of a din with the musical instruments. We couldn't, of course, sing freedom songs or anything of the sort. But we started making a hell of a clanging noise, you see. And the cops came up and said: "What's going on here!?"

We had one fellow who was a bit of a comedian, you know, he was a hell of a nice chap. That guy reckons: "Aw, hello baas. How you baas?"

The cop reckons: "Yes! What you want?"

"No baas we want to go to Johannesburg."

"Where's your permits?"

"Okay baas, we'll give you our permits now. Don't worry."

So the fellow walked into the police station itself. The lorries were parked outside, you see. Then this guy reckoned. "Heyyy, July handicap coming up very soon, hey."

Then the Dutchman, you know, the cop, said: "Yes. Got any tips?"

The fellow reckoned — huh — : "Definitely. I give you the tips, don't worry. Try this horse, definite winner. Try that horse, number two winner."

He gave him the *whole* lot. That cop was so dumb he take down the names of *all* the horses that guy gave him. Meantime it's a full card, you see. All this was to play for time and give us a chance to get on the cop's nerves.

By the time he, the comedian chap, finished he said: "Baas, man, we going for this wedding. Everybody's okay here. Come on, man. We're getting late for the wedding..." and all that.

Meantime we're busy making a din outside. So the cop reckons: "Okay. Don't make a noise, hey. All these people are sleeping here in Heidelberg. You mustn't make a noise. Please, you must go!"

We managed to get all three lorries through!■

From Heidelberg to Johannesburg there were no further problems for the delegation.

Chetty: Soon as we arrived, the Jo'burg comrades were looking for us, the five of us without permits. The Jo'burg comrades were Mosey Moolla and Babla Saloojee — I tell you, they were a tower of strength, eyyy, those guys were fantastic. You know, to organise that huge Congress of the People thing was no joke. So straight away, when the Natal Midlands delegation came through, they said: "We've got a tip-off the cops are looking for you five fellows."

So what do we do? "Doesn't matter, we'll send you somewhere." They sent us to some home, one of the TIC fellow's homes.

Later we were told everything's clear. So we could join our delegation. They had gone off to a cafe in Johannesburg, the Azad cafe or something. Hell, now that place is jampacked with delegations from everywhere. We find all our guys hustling for breakfast. The cafe-owner is just simply frying eggs, and cutting bread, heyyy. I tell you it was just simply chaotic in that place.

Now who's going to pay for all this? That

shopkeeper, the owner of the cafe says: "No, don't worry. The TIC is going to pay."

I passed the word around, saying: "Don't worry, the TIC is paying." The guys went to town on the bloody chow! The TIC must have had a hell of a heavy bill!

When we had finished there we drove off to Kliptown.

A view of the Congress of the People. Long and hard campaigning made this event possible.

VI. Kliptown, June 25 26th, 1955

19. The first day

The Congress of the People was held over two days in a field in Kliptown, just outside Johannesburg.

There had been bigger political meetings in South Africa, but the Kliptown gathering was and still is unique in our history. There were, according to the official figures announced at the Congress itself, 2 884 delegates present. We are speaking of *delegates,* not just spectators, as many of our informants insisted on reminding us.

Vandeyar: With a meeting like that, there were delegates in their thousands. I'm not talking about the masses coming to hear speakers. Every delegate there was a speaker. You know, if any one was called upon to say something he would be able to articulate his grievances, and say something about his plight in South Africa. That is the most inspiring thing of all. ■

Seven thousand spectators watched the proceedings. This was certainly the most representative gathering there has ever been in South Africa. It was a real people's parliament, with one difference. It was not, of course, sovereign. The first demand of the Charter that was to be adopted that weekend read: "The people shall govern." But in June 1955 the people did not (as they still do not) govern. The Congress of the People had to meet under the hostile shadow of the apartheid government's guns.

The Congress of the People was due to start soon

Young children, dressed in Congress uniform, welcome delegates to Kliptown.

after lunch, on Saturday the 25th of June.

Ellen Lambert (in 1955 she was Ellen Goss) secretary of the South African Coloured People's Organisation in the Transvaal, remembers:

Lambert: I woke up at four o'clock that morning. We were filled with excitement. Do you know what I wore that day? I wore khaki pants and a black, green and gold sweater. Those days it was unheard of for girls to wear pants!

87

Chetty: The crowds were coming in. We got there about 11 o'clock. The conference itself was going to start at three o'clock, half past two, something like that. And the crowds were pouring in, and pouring in. God, I tell you, by the time we were ready at three o'clock it was just a sea of heads.

You know, we couldn't understand where these people were coming from. Bus loads. Lorry loads. Motor cars. People walking by foot. They were coming from everywhere.

I said to our guys: "What's happening? Where's all these people coming from?" Mosey said: "These are all the delegates from the country." And you could see the guys were barefoot, you know, wearing blankets, others were wearing that zebra type uniform, also decently dressed guys, all types. ■

◀ "The crowds were pouring in, and pouring in" — A.S. Chetty. They arrived carrying posters reflecting the demands found in the Charter.

▲ A group of Indian women delegates led by Mrs Dadoo, mother of Dr Y.M. Dadoo. Since he was unable to attend due to a banning order, she accepted the Isitwalendwe Award on his behalf. The award, for contributing to the freedom struggle, was also made to Father Trevor Huddleston and Chief Albert Luthuli.

Delegates came from many different communities, proud of their different cultures, and proud of being South African.

▼ Delegates from various parts of the country march with their demands. This banner refers to the banning orders placed on many of the Congress leaders.

▼ High spirits marked the Congress of the People. As A.S. Chetty describes: "The singing was going on. Eating. Distribution of pamphlets. Reading. People talking. It was such a massive crowd."

Nair: When we reached the Congress there was a carnival atmosphere, in fact the organisation was immaculate, it was a very high standard. They had made provision for people who did not eat meat, soup with and without meat. Later in the Treason Trial, the police produced the placards announcing "SOUP WITHOUT MEAT".

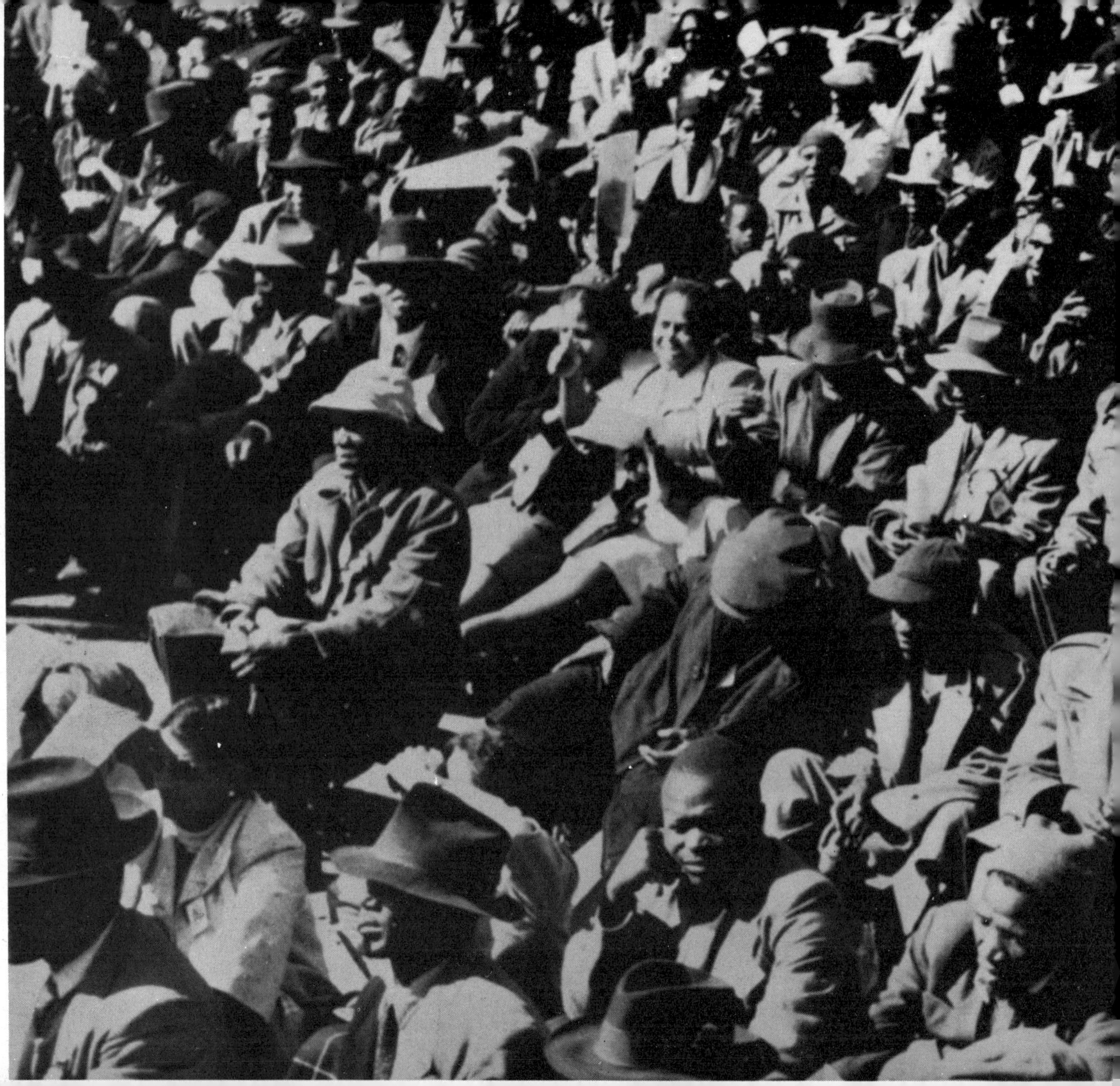

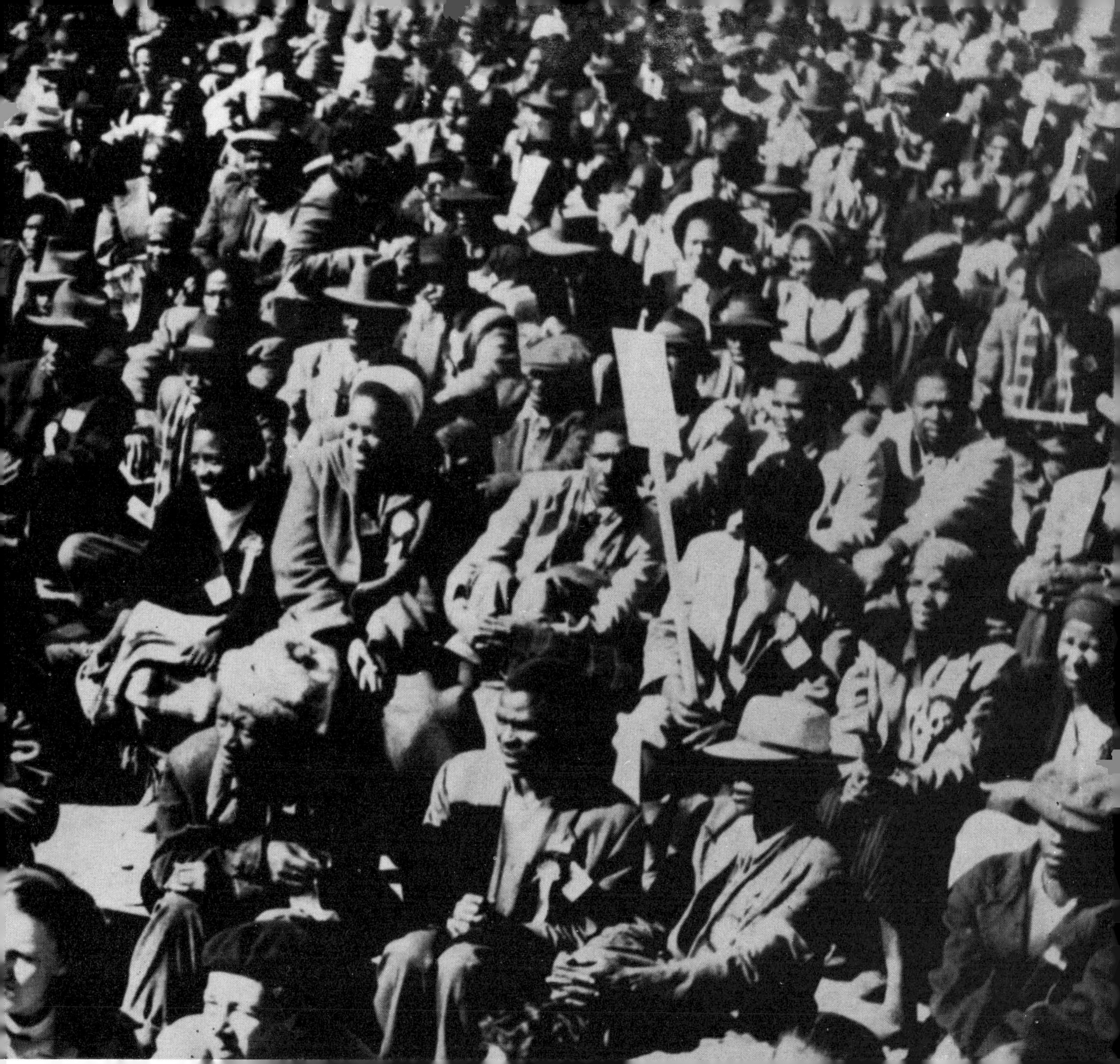

On the platform during one of the sessions.

Tshabangu: We were seated there, all of us. Two bricks, two bricks and a long plank. All of us were seated.

Ramokgadi: Well, man, it was a mass meeting. Thousands gathered there from all over the country, even from the rural areas. I really started to know how people were moved by the conditions under which we live.

Chetty: The Natal Midlands delegation sat right at the front, near the podium. From where we sat you could overlook the whole place. A sea of heads. The singing was going on. Eating. Distribution of pamphlets. Reading. People talking. It was such a massive crowd.

Then just after two, I think, they started the session. They had a band from Johannesburg, ANC guys, they played with a guitar, and they started singing. Eyy, I tell you the way they were singing, the whole crowd started joining in.

Then the conference went on proper. While the procedure was going on they interspersed with a little bit of singing. You know, Lilian Ngoyi and Winnie Mandela and Albertina, and they had somebody from the Cape, a Sacpo and a COD group rendering their items.

Every time a session of the Charter took place, then straight away silence and seriousness. Item by item the Charter was read. The National Consultative Committee had already prepared a draft. Then it was thrown open for discussion.

It was done so methodically. If anyone had an amendment then they came right up to the podium to the mike. Then, after, it was put to the house. Show your hands and all of that.

View of the platform at the Congress of the People.

Tshabangu: It continued the whole day. Speakers after speakers. It was my first time to see so many people in one place and saying one thing. All the speakers were saying different words, but meaning the same aim and object.

And the silence was there. Ten thousand people, but there was no coughing business. What was coming from the speaker's mouth everybody was thirsty to swallow that.

Lambert: It was the first great meeting that I attended, where I heard so many prominent speakers. I listened to all of them. ∎

One of those who spoke from the platform was none other than the legendary 'Lion of the East', Gert Sibande. We have already heard from interviewees the central role Sibande played in collecting demands from the rural areas of the Transvaal, particularly the Eastern Transvaal.

Today Gert Sibande is about 85 years old. He says he was born in 1901. He is in poor health and his memory fails him. As he says, "I do not remember in a straight line anymore".

This is what the Lion of the East told us about Kliptown.

Sibande: After I was banished to Evaton, I got a two-year banning order. It expired just before the Congress of the People. I knew that they would ban me again. But they couldn't find me. I was determined to go to Kliptown, because my name was down as a speaker.

I went to Kliptown wearing a disguise. I was wearing a balaclava and a jacket with the collar up around my neck. At Kliptown they were looking for me.

Gert Sibande, "Lion of the East", went to Kliptown in disguise because he was being hunted by the police.

Members of the Special Branch grouped together ▶ near the main gathering, took notes and observed carefully

I stood right next to Muller, head of the Special Branch. And then the chairman said: "I now call the next speaker." I walked up to the platform and a young man took off my disguise.

"It's Sibande, it's Sibande!" Muller shouted. The police rushed towards the platform and surrounded it. But then Muller said to them: "Go back to your cars." He knew that I was very powerful that time. If I would have said kill them (the police), the people would have killed them.

I took the platform for half an hour. I spoke about politics. If there is something serious in my heart, I can take two or three hours before I am finished. I was very hard that day. I am very powerful when I address a meeting. I never used notes. I always spoke from my head.

The police didn't serve the banning order that day. I slipped away.

20. The second day

On Sunday, June 26 1985 the apartheid government sent its own delegation in force to Kliptown.

Esakjee: It was a beautiful day. It was a perfect day. Probably I would say that God wanted this day, just to come. That's why He's giving the people a beautiful day. And while we're on it there was a *helluva* big sandstorm just before the police raided the place!

Tshabangu: In the morning of the second day it was Dr Letele, at that time he was staying in Kimberley. He was speaking on "All national groups shall have equal rights". It was that particular clause, and read by an intellectual. You could feel when he was speaking that this man, nê, he was polished from childhood.

After that, they asked: "Who accepts?" All the hands were up. Three thousand delegates. After that: "Those against?" Not a single one.

Chetty: The proceedings were practically over, then, all of a sudden we found the cops coming in. The guys were coming in truck loads.

Nyembe: Chief Luthuli had sent a letter to the South African government to send delegates to come. Late in the afternoon on Sunday, when we look around, we see 300 police with their horses. The people said that the South African government has now sent its delegates!

Tshabangu: Late in the afternoon, two hundred mounted policemen came. With horses, you know

Special Branch members took photographs of the proceedings

the horses, they jump, nê.

Matthews: All races were there. The government himself was invited to attend. What they did — the government delegation came very late, round about four!

Chetty: At first they came on horses, and in those military vans. We were used to that, so we didn't worry so much. But then after that, we got a little frightened when the saracens started arriving — you know those tanks?

I said to our guys: "Yeyy, I hope we don't get bombed here, yooh!"

They reckon: "No, don't worry."

Tshabangu: Our boldness which we had that day! I think even the lion is not more bold than us. When the horses were coming, no one ran away. We sat there looking at them.

Chetty: In military style the cops circulated the whole of the Kliptown ground. They stood with their sten guns. With military uniforms, camouflage uniforms, they circulated the whole thing.

Then this big chief, this cop, I don't know who he is, big size fellow too, he comes up to the podium, and he stops the proceedings. And he says: *"You all under arrest!"* In terms of certain, certain clause, this that and everything. *"Don't move!"*

Chetty: Hell-l-l…and you can imagine the tenseness at that time.

▼"You all under arrest!"

◀The public gallery of the Congress of the People.

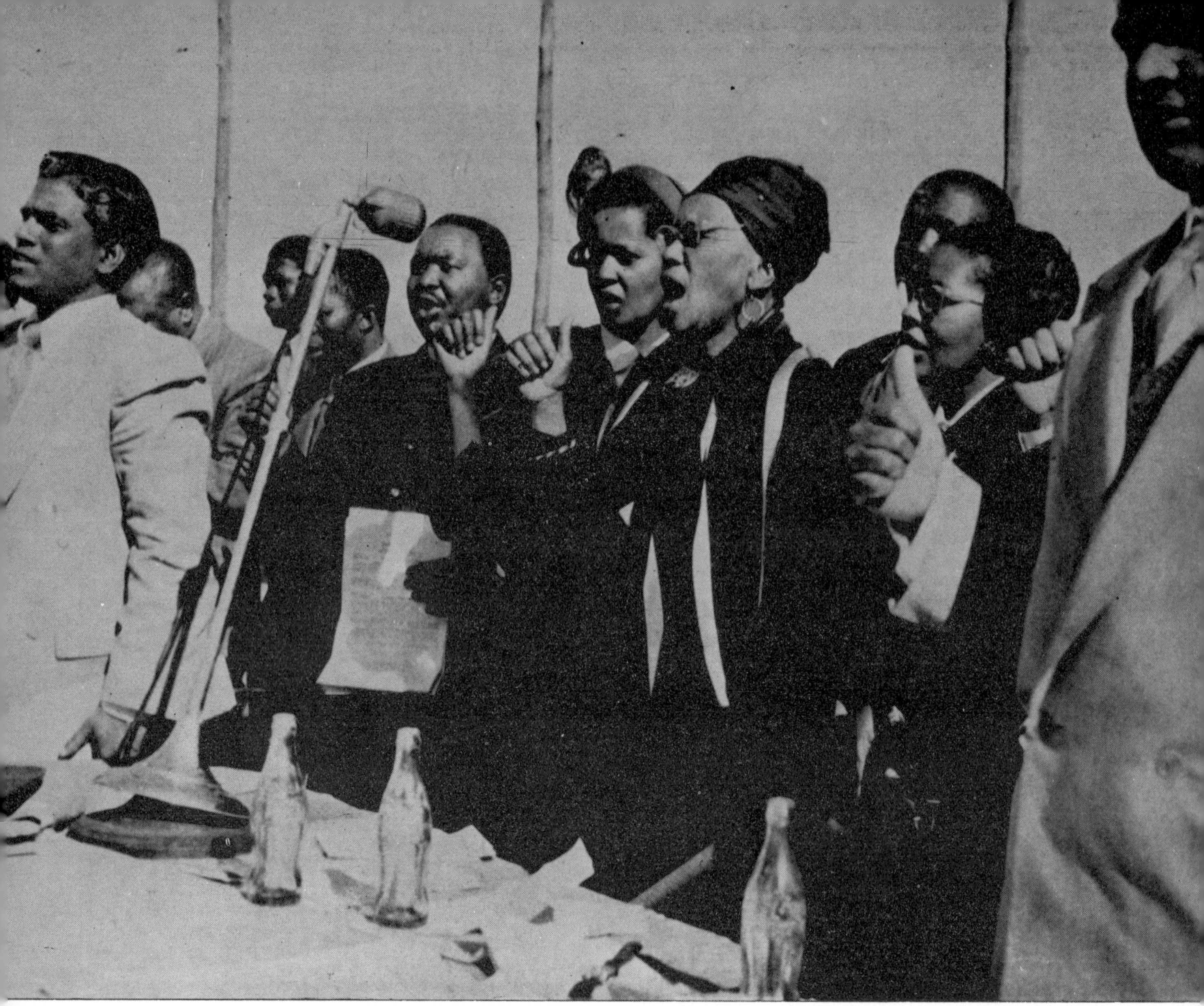

Chetty: And I tell you the crowd was just getting angry. They were prepared to retaliate and lose their lives in that place. The cops would have mowed us all down. Because these guys were at absolute readiness. All this big fellow had to do was give them the signal and they would have mowed us down.

So this huge sea of people, right. Next thing Ida Mtwana get on to that platform. And Ida said: "Comrades, this is the hour! Please do not do a thing! Let's start singing!" And she started singing. And this big cop couldn't do a thing. ∎

After singing the National Anthem, *Nkosi Sikelela iAfrika*, the delegates proceeded with the Congress, completing the final clauses of the Freedom Charter. This work was done with the gathering still surrounded by the police.

It seems that the police intended the Congress of the People to endorse the Freedom Charter.

Nair: For the very good reason that they wanted it to be adopted so it could be challenged in court. ∎

Philip Kgasago, a delegate from Mofolo, remembers how the delegates left the field at Kliptown.

Kgasago: At the end the square was surrounded by mounted police. They left one opening for everyone to go through. Then, as we dispersed, at the opening, there where people went out, we were searched of all documents. Every document was taken from us.

They were calling us one by one. Taking all, everything. All we had in our pockets, and everything. Putting them in big envelopes. Writing where you stay, addresses.

Nair: Practically every poster and document was snatched away, including posters saying *"Ladies This Way"*.

Chetty: Meantime, some cops were running around trying to catch some fellows and all that, and old Benston was taking a roll of film of the whole proceedings. They came to grab old Benston's camera. Next moment Babla [Saloojee] grabbed the camera, smuggled it into his overcoat, and he was over that fence and gone. That roll of film was saved. But they confiscated a lot of cameras and documents and all that. ∎

Zolly Malindi, currently president of the UDF Western Cape, was present on that day at Kliptown. He came to the opening where the police were processing the delegates. He had a copy of the Xhosa version of the Freedom Charter in his possession. When the mounted police surrounded the field, Zolly Malindi took off one of his shoes and socks and hid the Xhosa version of the Freedom Charter under his foot.

At the exit the police emptied his pockets, made him take off his shoes. But they forgot to make him remove his socks! And so the Xhosa version of the Freedom Charter was successfully smuggled out.

Later, after the Congress of the People, the Congress movement looked all over South Africa for the official Xhosa version. The police raid meant the loss of so many important documents.

◀ When the police arrived Ida Mntwana got on to the platform and led the Congress in a freedom song. "She said: 'Comrades this is the hour! Please do not do a thing!'...And this big cop couldn't do a thing."

The process of searching the delegates as they left took several hours.

Chetty: Leave your docket here, out you go. Leave your docket here, out you go. And so we were processed. When a cop starts writing, you know how long he takes! It finished after eight that night for the tail-enders.

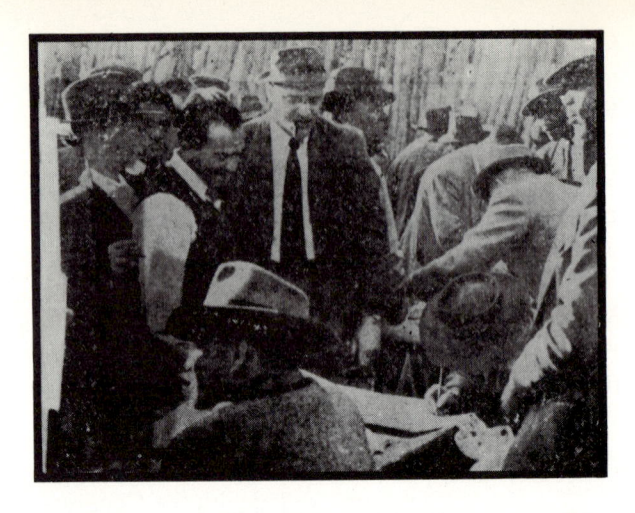

"Friendly search at the end of the Congress of the People" was the caption for this picture printed in *The Star* the following day.

VII. Reporting back

21. Conveying the message, house to house

The 26th June, 1955 did not mark the end of the Freedom Charter campaign. The task of delegates and volunteers now became one of reporting back and popularising the Charter.

Nair: After the Congress of the People, report back meetings were held in all the areas, at factory levels, and in fact, in all the affiliates of the Joint Congress organisations.

The task of all delegates was exactly that. They were pressed upon to do so at the Congress itself. They had to report back *and* go out, mobilising and organising.

Q: Were people satisfied with the Freedom Charter at the report backs, or were they disappointed?

Nair: Far from disappointment, at *all* the report back meetings that we had, the Freedom Charter was fully supported and wholly endorsed.

Tshabangu: From Kliptown it was our duty now to impart what we accepted, the Freedom Charter. I am one of those who took an active part conveying this message, house to house, where I stayed [Dube, Soweto]. I entered each and every house in my area for the Freedom Charter. I spread that gospel.

And I must say all the people accepted it, even those who had no membership with the mother body [ANC]. But automatically they felt that they were part and parcel of that movement.

It was in 1955. We could see now liberation, we could smell freedom in front of us.

Esakjee: There were report back meetings in every area. In Johannesburg, people went back. In the rural areas as well, especially where delegates come from. The delegates were sent a lot of literature, especially the Freedom Charter itself. We had report back meetings, big and small, on sports fields, homes, halls. ∎

In Durban Dorothy Nyembe remembers the main report back meeting being held at Currie's Fountain.
Q: How many people were at the meeting at Currie's Fountain?
Nyembe: Really, I don't remember. I can't tell a lie.
Q: A lot?
Nyembe: It was a full square, a full square.
Q: Thousands?
Nyembe: Thousands? Come! Thousands is nothing at Currie's Fountain. I know only that the place was full.

[Another informant tells us that when full, Currie's Fountain would hold perhaps 40 000.]

Some were standing on the road. Ja, the loudspeakers were put on all over, down there, so that even the person outside on the road can hear.
Ramokgadi: It was a most funny thing. When we read to the branches now what has been adopted they were definitely surprised. For example the branch in Alexandra heard the clause on houses and security and thought that it was their very own demand that had been adopted. When they heard that, no, everybody from different areas had brought this demand, they were definitely surprised. ∎

However, the quality of the reporting back seems to have been uneven. In a number of regions people

Elliott Tshabangu, veteran of many campaigns: "I entered each and every house in my area for the Freedom Charter. I spread that gospel."

we interviewed felt that more could have been done. This is what happened in Paarl:

Abrahams: I didn't get to Kliptown. A delegation from our [Food and Canning Workers' Union] branches went and then reported back. The delegates came home, and it were a bit 'finish and klaar'. That is my feeling about it. They bring the Freedom Charter back, and read and discuss a little. But it was not serious enough. ∎

Reggie Vandeyar, then living in Fordsburg, has a similar memory.

Vandeyar: All the Congresses obviously had report back meetings. But...well, I can only speak of the Transvaal Indian Congress. I think there was more discussion on the jubilation side of things than the actual report back. There was talk about the success of the meeting, how great this meeting was, the police harassment and what-not. We went on in this way for weeks on end! [Laughter.]

It was only ten years later that we realised how little work was put into propagating the Freedom Charter itself. In 1963 I was sent to Robben Island. In 1967 we initiated discussion on the Island. The Charter was the main theme of discussion. Little did we realise until then how little work was done by the organisations to propagate that great achievement. I mean in a concerted fashion.

Concerted work may have been done in some places, you know, in the Eastern Cape and elsewhere. But generally there was not sufficient propagation of the Charter.

But I don't want to slate our leadership of that period as being negligent. You know we are forgetting one important thing. The Treason Trial contributed to fragmenting the organisations. Then there were the Africanist rumblings. ∎

Groups of Five

In at least one centre the report backs and discussion of the Freedom Charter seem to have been conducted very thoroughly. This centre was Port Elizabeth.

One veteran who was active in the Korsten branch of the ANC spoke to us. He complains that his memory is not good and that he has not been given warning so that he can prepare himself. But he then gives us a detailed story, with dates accurate to the month, in perfect English.

Veteran: But I am not at all satisfied, because I find I omit some of the things I ought to tell you by not knowing the right grammar, the right verb, predicate, or anything like that. ∎

The comrade is not easy to reassure. But we press on. We ask him how he remembers the report back from the Congress of the People. This is his story:

Veteran: We called a public, open air meeting in an empty property. We could not use the council grounds, but in Korsten we had open properties without a house, which belonged to our people. So we used those sites as a meeting ground.

We used to lift the flag of the ANC and the people came themselves. We need not to tell them that today we have got a meeting. But people were always watching the place where we used to gather. When they saw the flag the people knew there is something cropping. They came hurrying, coming to hear.

So we read the Freedom Charter, from the first clause to the tenth clause. I think the last clause reads: "There will be harmony and friendship"... I think, I forget it (it is many, many years since I read it)...no wait..."There will be peace and friendship and harmony." Other clauses read, like, ah, I think the first clause reads: "All the people are equals in the face of God. Equality is being practised in heaven". ■

In Port Elizabeth discussion of the contents of the Freedom Charter, clause by clause was more advanced and reached a wider range of people than anywhere else.

What made this mass education work possible was the organisational structures in the townships of Port Elizabeth. Here, like nowhere else, the famous M (for Mandela)-Plan had been implemented.

Ngoyi: At this time I was the contact in the Kwazakele branch of the ANC. There were also contacts in New Brighton, and so on. There was an executive of six members. They would prepare reading material and send it out to zones. The zones were made up of streets, with a small group in each street, and a group leader.

The ANC was so strong in the Eastern Cape. This was because it had political study groups, it kept people up to date all the time. And it had this zoning system, which meant that it could penetrate right down to the street. People were politicised who had never entered the door of a school. ■

William Fanti remembers the Freedom Charter being discussed in these small groups.
Fanti: The Freedom Charter was read in meetings, and the audience was given copies of the Charter.

We were also lectured about the Freedom Charter, what the meaning of it was. But this was done in *small* meetings.

It was decided, because of developments, not to call big meetings. Because security was being tightened up. So small groups on different days discussed the Charter, until the organisation was banned.

There were branches in all the townships. But these branches were broken down into *small* groups. A group of five, you know. We organised street by street. This group of five was listening to a lecture. Then one person from this group is taking the lecture to another area, to lecture some people there. Explaining the matter. The people would then pose their questions. Then that second group takes this lecture and one of them delivers it to a third group. And so forth, and so forth.

Eating the Charter

To popularise the Freedom Charter a campaign to collect one million signatures endorsing the Charter was launched. Elliott Tshabangu remembers going house to house in Dube, Soweto to collect signatures. In other centres it was mainly at meetings that signatures were collected.

In Cape Town there were regular Sunday meetings on the Grand Parade.
Abrahams: Every, every Sunday a mass meeting, if it were not Sactu then it were CPC, or whoever. Hooo, we were busy those days! We would drive a lorry under the big tree, and use the lorry for a platform. A lot of people would come to those meetings. The Parade was full. ■

One Sunday, at a Sactu rally, volunteers were at the Parade to collect names, addresses and signatures on the back of the Freedom Charter. Frances Baard, a Sactu stalwart from Port Elizabeth, was in Cape Town for the rally.

Baard: I remember one time after that [Kliptown], we were in Cape Town, talking to some people about the Freedom Charter, so that they would know that thing. ■

Eileen van der Vindt was also at the Parade that day.

Van der Vindt: My friend and I were standing there in the Parade getting people to sign copies of the Charter. Suddenly the police arrived.

Baard: One of the girls who was with me there was carrying her Freedom Charter with her, and there comes the security. They came up to her....

Van der Vindt: The policeman wanted to get the signature form with the Freedom Charter from my friend. So she swallowed it, quick.

Baard: She ate it, that policeman couldn't get a thing out of that....

Van der Vindt: But the newspaper snapped a photo. And there she was, next Sunday, front page of the *Golden City Post*...having just chewed the Charter.

The target of one million signatures was not to be achieved. Barely one tenth of that number were collected. Speaking to activists of that time it is clear that other campaigns, often defensive campaigns against the onslaught of the apartheid government, came increasingly to occupy people's energies.

"And there she was, next Sunday, front page of the *Golden City Post* .....having just chewed the Charter".

VIII.
Rumblings within

22. "Congress has something up its sleeve"

After the Congress of the People there were rumblings within the ANC related to certain ideological differences over the Freedom Charter.

The ANC adopted the Freedom Charter at its national conference in March 1956. There were, however, rumblings in certain quarters. According to Chief Albert Luthuli: "Congress did not unanimously adopt the Charter, though the majority was large. But our extreme right-wing [the Africanists, now independently led by Mr Robert Sobukwe] dismissed it *in toto*. Their compromising [sic] stand made discussion very difficult. [1]

The Africanists had problems with the opening of the preamble of the Charter: "South Africa belongs to all who live in it, black and white...." They argued that South Africa belongs by right only to the original African inhabitants.

In Natal and the Cape some elements within the ANC felt that the economic clauses of the Charter went too far. Billy Nair talks about these rumblings.

Nair: The ANC adopted the Charter as an organisation at its 1956 Congress. They called a special conference to discuss the problem that arose when certain elements in the ANC felt that the Charter had gone a bit too far, you know, on the land question. Some of these guys were small landowners — from Durban — that caused the trouble.

Robert Mangaliso Sobukwe, who led the Africanist breakaway.

Q: Were these PAC people or Natal ANC?
Nair: Natal ANC, and you had certain elements in the Transvaal too, who later broke from the ANC to form the PAC. That was in '58. Now, they too felt like the state at the time of the Treason Trial, that the Charter was a socialist document.
Q: A combination of a sort of radicalism in relation to whites — wanting to "kick them out", but conservative economically, presumably?
Nair: Ja. They felt, in the case of the PAC, that the white man had no place whatsoever...in a future South Africa, and that they had to be thrown out — they had to be thrown into the sea. ∎

In the Cape too there were some within the ANC who were unhappy with the economic clauses of the Charter.
Veteran: In Cape there were people like Z.K. Matthews that were not happy with the clause of nationalising the means of production.
Q: That's interesting, because the idea for the Congress of the People came from Z.K. Matthews!
Veteran: Yes. The idea outgrew his way of thinking, it went further than he thought!∎

As early as December 1955 *Drum*[2] magazine detected some of these rumblings and had this to say:

Congress has something up its sleeve!

Conflicting constructions have been put on the silence the African National Congress continues to keep on its plans for the next phase of the struggle against racial oppression. Most people think that Congress has been paralysed by the bans while a few are convinced that Congress has something up its sleeve. The Police, too, if the recent raids are any

113

guide, seem to think Congress is up to something.

It is true that up to a certain point the bans on the movements of the key Congressmen and the prohibition of unauthorised meetings in African areas, coupled with the absence of a sympathetic Press, have slowed down Congress activity. But this is only part of the story. What is also happening at the moment is that the leaders of the African National Congress are trying to shape African mass enthusiasm for non-violence into a pliable weapon for use when the time is ripe for the next phase of that struggle. This is an exceedingly complicated job, as will soon be shown...

...One of the reasons for this is that Congressmen are not of one mind on the form of the next phase...

...Four different forces are at work competing for the friendship of the African...The Leftists have staked a very strong claim for a Marxist basis. So much so that when Professor Matthews's suggestion of a Magna Carta and a convention was translated in to the Congress of the People there was introduced into the Freedom Charter the principle of nationalisation — something which commits the African National Congress as one of the sponsors of the Congress of the People to a new economic principle. From the Centre have come the liberals. For them partnership can be established only on a liberal democratic basis.

There still remain two relatively new forces which compete for the loyalties of the African. The first of these is African Irredentism. It teaches that the people of Africa belong together and as such should stand together against White domination on the African continent. The logical goal of the Irredentists is 'Africa for the Africans'.

The second force in this category is composed of those who see in the ideal of a common destiny for the men of colour in the world the only hope for the African. As a result they work for closer bonds between the peoples of Asia and those of Africa...

...In the meantime much depends on the outcome of the quarrel between the Centre and the Left in Congress over the Freedom Charter as it stands. The Charter, it will be remembered, was adopted by the Kliptown congress. There is a barely concealed cleavage on what adoption then implied. The Left insists that adoption bound the sponsoring bodies to accept the Charter as their own and straight away proceed to press for its being signed by a million people before it is ratified by the sponsoring bodies' national conferences. These tactics are designed to place the African National Congress in the position where its Centre wing will be confronted at the national conference with the accomplished fact of nationalisation having been accepted and the Charter signed by a million people — some, better still, most of them, Congressmen.

The Centre takes the view that adoption of the Charter at Kliptown was merely acknowledgement of its existence. To be binding on the sponsoring bodies it had to be ratified by the national conferences of the sponsoring bodies, after which it could be signed.

The real significance of the tactics of the Left lies in their being calculated to place Mr. Luthuli (a known Centre man) and his personal followers in an extremely awkward position. He has stated publicly that he would sooner resign from the Congress presidency than see this body turn in the Communist direction. It remains to be seen what he will do if the national conference of the African National Congress, which meets in December, decides that the nationalisation of industry, the mines and the banks — as demanded in the Freedom Charter — is the new Congress line." ∎

The *Drum* article, while putting its finger on some of the debates occuring within the ranks of the ANC, overrated the strength of those opposing the Charter. As we have noted, the ANC conference in March 1956 adopted the Charter by a large majority, and Chief Luthuli threw his weight behind it. In Luthuli's words: "The Charter produced in Kliptown is, line by line, the direct outcome of conditions which obtain — harsh, oppressive and unjust conditions. It is thus a practical and relevant document."[3]

Luthuli qualifies this view, however, by adding: "The Freedom Charter is open to criticism. It is by no means a perfect document. But its motive must be understood, as must the deep yearning for security and human dignity from which it springs."[4]

But for Luthuli the major significance of the Charter was the broad impact that the actual Freedom Charter campaign had: "Nothing in the history of the liberatory movement in South Africa quite caught the popular imagination as this did, not even the Defiance Campaign. Even remote areas were aware of the significance of what was going on."[5]

This slogan on the wall of a bank refers to one of the clauses of the Freedom Charter that provoked the Africanist breakaway from the ANC.

The people demonstrated their loyalty when the leadership of the Congress movement was charged with treason.

IX.
The Treason Trial

23. "The Charter was in the front line now"

The apartheid government was frightened by the vision of the Freedom Charter. In December 1956, 156 Congress leaders were arrested and charged with treason.

The police raid on the final day of the Congress of the People was the prelude to a massive treason trial. On 5 December 1956, beginning at 4 a.m., police arrested leaders of the Congress Alliance in all parts of South Africa. The accused, at first numbering 156, reflected the multi-racial composition of the Alliance. Amongst those arrested were Chief Albert Luthuli, Nelson Mandela, Oliver Tambo, Joe Slovo, Moses Kotane, Ahmed Kathrada, Duma Nokwe, Helen Joseph and Ruth First.

They were accused of participating in a 'countrywide conspiracy', inspired by international communism, to overthrow the state by violence. The state used the Freedom Charter as part of its evidence. According to one of the 156 accused, Prof Z.K. Matthews, the state charged that "drafting and adopting the Freedom Charter was an overt act of High Treason, part of a plot to overthrow the state by violence"[1].

The atmosphere of a military operation was created by carefully coordinated air transport of the accused to Johannesburg from the various centres.

Ultimately charges were withdrawn against all but 30 of the accused. In March 1961, the Special Criminal Court set up to hear the case acquitted all, holding that the policy of the Congress Alliance, including the Freedom Charter, had not been to overthrow the state by violence or to replace the existing order with a dictatorship of the proletariat.

The trial was characterised by mass popular support for the accused, manifested in demonstrations and in extensive financial assistance. Amongst the defence team that secured their acquittal was Abram Fisher QC.

Elliott Tshabangu remembers the feelings of the people at the time.

Tshabangu: When the treason came in '56, we used to sing that, nê, *Umzima Lomthwalo* — this burden is heavy. This treason, it was no joke, but we didn't retreat. We were active beyond the limit of active. The Charter was in the front line now.

To support the trialists we moved up and down, up and down. We contributed the last money we were getting. Every week, pay so much. It was often so little, but we managed to do that.

Our leaders were behind the fence, but they were not shivering. They were ordinary men and women behind bars, but they were not afraid.

That is why we composed a slogan: "We stand by our leaders". When our leaders were coming for the trial here at the Drill Hall, here in this area in Twist Street you could see thousands surrounding all over. Everyone just to see a glance of our leaders.

People had no fear, people of that time, you follow, because the message of the Freedom Charter was already spread. The Charter was a magnet beckoning the masses. The Freedom Charter was that thing to us. ■

Chief Albert Luthuli, president of the ANC was one of the accused in the Treason Trial. Here he chats during a break in the trial. After four long years he and all the accused were acquitted.

After the Congress of the People hundreds of thousands of copies of the Charter in all the languages of the people were distributed. Here is an invoice of a Johannesburg order.

X
The Charter lives on

24. A goatskin tobacco pouch

Despite all attempts, the apartheid government has never been able to remove the Freedom Charter from the people's memory. Down the years the demands of the Charter, and the very document itself have surfaced — often in surprising places.

The early 1960s saw a fierce onslaught against the mass organisations.

Thousands who had taken part in the Congress of the People campaign and in the wider activities of the Congress Alliance went to jail. Many, in fact most of those we interviewed for this book, were imprisoned at this time. Some went to jail for extremely long spells, 15, 17, 20 years.

But the Freedom Charter was not erased from the minds of oppressed and democratic South Africans. As the following story confirms, it remains part of the lives of all who suffer under apartheid, wherever they are, whether they live in the towns or bantustans.

Christmas Tinto remembers:

Tinto: In 1965, when I came from Robben Island to the Transkei I found my house demolished by Matanzima and Vorster's bulldozers. Anyway. There was an opposition chap to the Transkeian thing, he was an old member of the ANC. Ja. Now when I arrived there he said: *"Thanks* comrade that you are here. We have got a meeting in another area. Matanzima is going to address those people about the Trust scheme. He is going to tell them to accept the Trust. Now I want you to lead the people in asking questions to Matanzima and his ministers."

And I said: "Okay. But organise a broken overall

and a broken hat."

He organised it.

There was another comrade who was from Johannesburg. We both wore overalls. We came *very* early in the morning. In those meetings people are sitting on the ground outside. They call it, that meeting, *imbizo*, ja, it's a tribal gathering.

Now, I said: "First of all, okay, this sun is going to be hot. Let's sabotage Matanzima and his crew, my comrade. Now we must put the chairs on *that* side. Matanzima must look to the sun. The people must be on this side."

He said: "Okay!"

We put the chairs and tables there.

Now I said to this comrade: "We must make a big noise as if we are a hundred, but we are only two. You must sit *there*, and I sit here. I will do the tough questioning and then when I sit down, you stand up over there and Matanzima must see it is a lot of people, but we are only two."

Anyway, *there* the cars are coming now. It was Kaizer Matanzima, it was the Minister Madikizela, it was the magistrate, it was the interpreter, it was two policemen, a C.I.D. and an ordinary policeman in uniform. They were six, they sit there.

Now, we were taught in this way in the ANC, that if you go to such meetings you must be the *first* to do the questioning. Don't let a person stand up first, because people will go with *that* person. When you come up with the right thing all the hearts and minds of the people will have already gone on that wrong journey. You must *first* jump up.

Now, I had my small pocketbook. I was ready.

Kaizer Matanzima stood up and said: "Tembus! The South African government is honouring you to have your children educated." Matanzima was trying to excuse the Trust scheme by saying it was a way to get children to school. "Having the cattle fenced in will mean that your children will go free to school."

Matanzima, when he was talking, was talking English. This chap was interpreting into Xhosa. I think they wanted the *magistrate* to hear what they were saying, because I can see no point of Matanzima speaking English. [Com T shakes his head, and clicks his tongue.]

Matanzima sat down, this white magistrate stood up and tried to speak Xhosa to say the same thing which Matanzima is saying. "This luck I am bringing you, I know it will be accepted by people with broad minds."

Now I jump up. I just saw that I must change this thing of greetings. The people in the homelands, whoever stood up to speak, first he will greet Matanzima in a way that he's big, *ahhh!* and praise with a name.

Now I stood up and said: "Mister Chairman." [Com T laughs in recollection.] "Ladies and gentlemen, if there *are* any ladies, although I see no ladies here, but I am sorry if there are no ladies here." I said that in Xhosa. That time, Matanzima, the sun is sitting to him. [Com T shades his eyes and peers and peers, mimicking Matanzima.] He wanted to see my face, and all he could see was the overall is broken, broken.

Anyway, I said: "People, I am not going to refer to the table there. I am going to ask *you,* all of you, three questions. If that table there answers these three questions, you must allow him to put his Trust here. One question (I would like the interpreter to

123

write these questions). This first one, today Hendrik Frensch Verwoerd is the fifth or fourth Prime Minister in this country. You are telling us to accept that they are going to build schools, and fence the places where the cattle eat. But today, as you are promising that, we have got more jails than schools. What is going to make us believe you are saying the truth by so saying? This government, up to this Verwoerd of today, he never make anything for the black people.

"Secondly, second question. The gentleman, *mister* Matanzima is speaking English, which means he is educated. Where did he learn English? Why are fences now suddenly needed for education? Where were the fences when he got educated?"

Now Matanzima *jump* up, and say: "Excuse me. There's a jackal which is wearing a skin of a sheep here. There's a jackal. This meeting is no good."

The people started shouting at Matanzima: "Sit down! Sit down! Mr President, sit down! The man has asked us to bring three questions. He has not finished his questions."

Matanzima said: "I won't be part of this meeting. I am going to close this meeting."

Now, I have not forgotten. [Com T laughs] I am coming to the Freedom Charter. Matanzima left. Then the people from the rural areas held me up. An old man said to the young people: "Look, we want people like this one who are not afraid of Matanzima. You must ask Matanzima the same questions if he comes back again, because this young man (that was me) is going back to work in Cape Town again. You must say *hamba* [go] Matanzima."

This old man then said: "Look here." (You know the skin of a goat, sewed, to make a tobacco pouch for the upper arm.) The old man said: "Bring me that needle." It was a long needle. He used the needle on his tobacco pouch on his arm. He bring out, bring out, a *very* small, small thing like this, a very small paper. And, he opened it, he opened it, he opened it. [Com T makes unfolding motions.]

He called another one. He said: "Read this to the people." Ja. When I looked at it, it's the Freedom Charter in Xhosa!

Then the old man said: "You must know this, the people of this country have decided on these lines. Read it to them."

Ja. I was surprised. He had kept it, that Freedom Charter, for ten years in his skin bag, there in Baziya district, Transkei.

B. UNDERSTANDING THE CHARTER

Today the ideas of the Freedom Charter are being revived. Poems, posters, pamphlets and banners have been produced popularising the Charter as a guide in numerous campaigns. At a meeting to save ANC guerillas from the gallows, Mrs Mosololi, mother of Jerry Mosololi, who was hanged in 1983 speaks. Next to her is Helen Joseph, veteran of the Congress of the People campaign.

Xl. What type of document is the Freedom Charter?

25. The Freedom Charter — the People's Charter

Many discussions on the Freedom Charter have centred around the question of what kind of document it is. Some have argued that it is a document of 'bourgeois democratic' demands. Others have said it is 'socialist'. How are we to understand the Charter?

We have tried to trace the process through which the Freedom Charter was created. Immediately after its adoption the state brought charges of high treason against 156 leading democrats. The charge of treason was based, in large measure, on the allegation that the Freedom Charter was a blueprint for a dictatorship of the proletariat. Africanists also attacked the Freedom Charter as importing 'foreign' socialist ideologies.

In our own time the Charter has been attacked as bourgeois or petit-bourgeois (that is, as primarily addressing the needs of the wealthy or professionals, small traders and so on, rather than the workers). Alternatively, it has sometimes been defended as a socialist document.

Our view is that the Charter is a people's document. It was created through a democratic process, unprecedented in this country and probably in most other countries of the world. It continues to speak to the interests of all oppressed South Africans who suffer under apartheid, and it wins support from democrats who struggle to end racial oppression and class exploitation.

The character of the Charter is not the result of any one original thinker nor even a group of people with fine intellects. Its content derives from the conditions under which the black people live in South Africa. In the first place, the Freedom Charter is a response to the denial of self-determination. In consequence of not controlling their own destiny, all blacks, but especially Africans, endure national oppression. All blacks, irrespective of class, are victims of this oppression. It is not only black workers, but all blacks who are disenfranchised and endure disabilities in almost every aspect of their lives.

One of the peculiarities of the South African society is that written into its structure is this systematic national oppression of all blacks. It is one of the factors that facilitates capitalist exploitation in South Africa. National oppression and capitalist exploitation are inextricably interlinked. In combination they ensure higher rates of profits than those found in most other parts of the world. The demands for the nationalisation of the key monopolies, and for the transfer of the land to those who work it, need to be seen in this light.

Socialist ideas were held by many, but not all, of those involved actively in the Congress of the People campaign. The idea of socialism had also begun to be spread widely in the 1950s through mass education and agitation. But the economic clauses in the Freedom Charter are not specifically socialist. They need to be seen in the context of a struggle for national liberation and self-determination. These demands derive, in part, from the historical basis of South African society, where nearly all the country's land has been seized from the original inhabitants. On the basis of this colonial robbery a new capitalist order was built. But over the years the wealth made by the collective efforts of all South Africans has been disproportionately enjoyed by the white minority. Within this white minority, the small but increasingly powerful monopoly capitalist group, controlling the mines, banks, and other major industries, has extracted vast wealth from the labour of millions of working-class South Africans.

This extraction of wealth has been closely tied in with a whole system of controls involving the national oppression of the majority. Pass laws, influx control, bantustans, racist labour bureaux — these measures have all assisted the super-exploitation of the African working class and the accumulation of great wealth. This wealth in turn goes to pay for further oppression.

As we have already said, the Charter is not a socialist document, but it *is* anti monopoly-capital. Any programme to end racial oppression in South Africa has to attack the key power centres of capitalism with which racial oppression is so interlocked.

It is incorrect to describe the Freedom Charter as a document of bourgeois democratic rights. Such a description rests on a number of errors. It is true that some of the demands made in the Charter, like the right of all adults to vote, or the right to organise trade unions, exist in western, capitalist democracies.

This shows that such rights are not impossible under capitalism. It would, however, be a grave error to imagine there was something inherently 'bourgeois' about these rights. In some societies the development of capitalism was made possible by popular struggles led by the bourgeoisie against feudalism. These popular struggles often led to revolutions in which the broad working masses made gains in terms of democratic rights. The extent to which such rights were extended reflected in all cases the degree of participation of the working class, peasantry and middle strata in these struggles.

Such democratic rights, even in the long-established western bourgeois democracies such as Britain and France, are not stable and uncontested. Often the rights are more formal than actual. Often the new ruling class seeks to restrict these rights. At the moment, Thatcherism in Britain is attacking the long-established democratic rights of the trade unions. Insofar as democratic rights are to be found in the western democracies, it has everything to do with the struggles and vigilance of the broad working masses in those countries.

Here in South Africa, capitalism has been developed without a popular democratic revolution. At first, it was British money and a British army of occupation that created the conditions for capitalist development. South Africa has long been a fairly advanced capitalist country. It is not as though we are still waiting to 'complete' the bourgeois capitalist stage of our development. For this very reason the democratic rights demanded in the Freedom Charter have nothing to do with 'completing' the bourgeois revolution in South Africa. Winning the democratic demands of the Freedom Charter will be a large step forward in building popular control of our country.

The Charter is also anti-imperialist. In the first place its attack on the monopolies is in part an attack on the control of the South African economy by international capital. Equally, in the present context, the clause demanding the right to work is an attack on foreign-controlled industries, for international investment is primarily concentrated in capital intensive industries, which, especially in the current recession, have thrown many people out of work.

But the Charter is also anti-imperialist in a more fundamental sense. For it is only when the people *do* govern that they can create the conditions to control their own country, make it fully independent and sovereign, and ensure that they break the stranglehold of international imperialism.

If it is correct to describe the Charter as a people's document, as a programme of a people struggling for self-determination, then we are considering a document that seeks to win the support of all those who oppose apartheid, all classes and strata who have an interest in its destruction.

XII. To whom does South Africa belong?

26. "South Africa belongs to all who live in it, black and white...."

Racist governments in South Africa have always attempted to exclude the black majority. Africans have been confined to a tiny portion of the territory and they have been treated as foreigners in the land of their birth. Against these practices the Freedom Charter proclaims that "South Africa belongs to all who live in it." Yet this statement has sometimes been criticised.

One of the goals of apartheid policy has been to divert African political aspirations away from the key political institutions of the South African state and into the bantustans. With a view to denying that Africans have any moral or legal right to a political voice in their own country, recent refinements of this policy strip African people of their South African citizenship.

Against such attempts of the apartheid state to define the African people as non-South Africans, to separate black from white and to divide blacks amongst themselves, the Charter declares that "South Africa belongs to all who live in it, black and white...."

What this means is that those who support the Charter seek no revenge against whites, that they seek a democratic South Africa where all can realise their aspirations.

Yet it is this very clause that evokes continued opposition from the supporters of black consciousness, who echo the opposition of the Africanists of the fifties. "To whom does Afrika belong...? it has been asked.

"Do stolen goods belong to a thief and not to their owner?"[1]

"It is an historical fallacy to say South Africa belongs to everybody: both oppressor and oppressed, robber and robbed. Azania is not a prostitute that belongs to everybody all the time..."[2]

It is true that the indigenous Khoisan and African people were violently dispossessed of their land over the two and a half centuries prior to Union, and that the Union of South Africa was founded amongst other things on this robbery.

Yet it is wrong to imply that the stolen land was appropriated by all whites. This is part of a wider tendency in some black consciousness thinking, to suggest that all whites are exploiters, and all blacks members of the working class. One does not therefore cooperate politically with any white, for that would be an alliance with one's slave-master.

In regard to the land, the truth is that the overall majority of landholdings in South Africa are controlled by a small group of monopolists. The small white farmers are themselves being squeezed off the land and there is ever increasing consolidation amongst the few big landholders.

It is, therefore, historically incorrect to suggest that the land grabbed from blacks, was robbed by and is held by all whites. Equally, while it is true that it is primarily the labour-power of blacks that has built South Africa, whites have also made a contribution. Present-day South Africa has been created by the common labour of all its people. The cities, factories, mines and agriculture have resulted from the energies of all South Africans. Though the wealth that is at present in the hands of a small minority of the whites, would be shared by the people, the Charter holds that all those who love South Africa, who consider it their home, who have contributed to building it and are prepared to continue to develop the country as a democratic, non-racial state, are part of South Africa.

"South Africa belongs to all who live in it, black and white." Azaso, Nusas and Cosas leadership share a platform, demonstrating the non-racial unity on which the democratic struggle is based.

Recent years have seen the emergence of a variety of creative forms of expression — songs, posters, banners and many more. People have drawn on traditional forms and past traditions of struggle. By integrating these with the new, the process of creating a democratic South African culture has been advanced.

XIII.
The Charter, the national question and culture

27. One people, many cultures.

The Congress of the People at Kliptown was not only a political event. It was a major cultural milestone. For the first time delegates from South Africa's many, diverse cultures came together, in their thousands, united behind a common vision. The Freedom Charter recognises both this desire for unity and the rich, cultural diversity of our country.

One of the key clauses of the Charter is headed: "All national groups shall have equal rights". It is crucial, yet it is also controversial. Some people have argued that this clause envisages the creation of four nations — whites, Africans, coloureds and Indians, or that it works on the basis that there are already four nations in South Africa.

Now it is unfortunate that the Charter uses the word 'national' in two different ways. In this clause it appears to be referring to distinct population groups, Africans, coloureds, Indians and whites. But in the sentence "The national wealth of our country, the heritage of all South Africans, shall be restored to the people", the word 'national' refers to all South Africans.

Lionel Forman, a leading white democrat who died in 1959, once advocated a multi-nation theory.[1] But neither this nor the so-called four nation theory has ever been adopted as a policy within the Congress movement or in our own time by the contemporary democratic movement. This theory survives not in the Charter itself nor amongst its supporters but mainly in polemical writings against it and the democratic movement as a whole.[2]

But what this clause of the Charter deals with (read together with the clause headed "The doors of learning and culture shall be opened") is of considerable significance. It calls for equality in the courts, bodies of state and schools, equal language rights and the right of all people to "develop their own folk culture and customs". While most people accept equality in bodies of state, courts and schools, the demand for language rights and the right to develop culture and customs is embarrassing to some. They feel that we are here adopting some of the worst elements of Verwoerdian cultural policy, the artificial or romantic preservation of tribal or pseudo-tribal cultures.

Such a view is both wrong and chauvinistic. At present there are two 'official' languages in South Africa, that is, the mother tongues of some 15 percent of the population are official languages for all. This state of affairs is characteristic of colonial-type conditions. In such situations an imperial power arrives and declares its law to be the law of the land and its language(s) official. One of the conditions for national liberation is equality in this sphere as in all others.

This is not to suggest that all elements of African culture or that of any other section of our population are necessarily progressive and worthy of preservation and encouragement. Just as some aspects of working-class culture are reactionary, a democratic policy would not encourage racist, sexist or chauvinistic aspects of any culture. It would encourage those developments that are compatible with the overall democratic, unifying and egalitarian content of the Charter. In order to protect these rights, according to the Charter, all apartheid laws and practices are to be abolished. The expression of apartheid ideas, anticipating developments in international law, is made a punishable crime.[3]

The clause calling for all national groups to have equal rights must be understood, in the first place, by considering what exists in contemporary South Africa. Insofar as apartheid denies people equal rights, it seeks to maintain this situation not only through coercion, but also through ideological domination, through trying to persuade the oppressed people to see themselves in a particular way, in a manner that facilitates their oppression. Through declaring black cultures to be worthless or through reviving them in an artificial, static manner, it is sought to breed self-contempt in blacks, to immobilise them in the face of the apparently superior white culture. To achieve national liberation requires the development of a democratic African culture. This would not be an exclusivist, racial culture, but would rather be the precondition for the development of all other cultures.

28. Mzwakhe: "Culture must be a weapon"

Mzwakhe, a popular poet, is UDF Transvaal media officer. He is also secretary of the Khuvangano Cultural Group and director of an experimental play called "Abasebenzi". Here he talks about the role of 'cultural workers'.

When the charter was drawn,
A vision of a true society was born.
A dark cloud giving way to the blue sky.
The freedom wagon moved with direction.
Yes, the people's agenda was adopted.

On this 30th anniversary of the Freedom Charter, cultural workers should also take stock of their presence in the struggle. On the same wavelength one must submit that the type of opposition cultural workers are facing, like other democrats, is formidable although not indestructible. Facing the same oppressions (passes, poverty, the risk of jail) cultural workers also have a special duty to struggle in the field of ideas.

On television, on the radio, in the press, in the church and in the classroom the people are bombarded with a massive proliferation of ideas that seek to harmonise them with subjugation. It is for this reason that the progressive movement inside the country must mobilise the fraternity of cultural workers to counter this threat. In doing this we can build upon the heritage of struggle and resistance culture.

Racial, colonial and imperialist domination all involve cultural oppression and attempt, either directly or indirectly, to do away with the most militant and vital elements of culture of the subjected people. But our people have been able to keep their culture alive despite continual and organised repression of their cultural life, and because they continued to resist cultural oppression even when their early politico-military resistance was destroyed.

Culture is a fundamental element of history in any given society. It is a product of history just like the flower is the product of a plant.

For us culture must be a weapon that we use effectively to raise the awareness of the people about their living conditions and the reasons for their sufferings. Through it we can engage a wide spectrum in the political process, and develop active workers for the liberation movement.

Culture permeates all aspects of our national struggle, be it workers demanding better conditions and fair wages, students demanding that the doors of learning be flung wide open, or community organisations fighting high rents.

As we take stock of our performances we should make a solemn pledge that if we are playwrights then our plays will carry a message of hope that we shall be free in our life-time; if we are poets, the beauty of poetry won't be determined by its rhyme and rhythm but by the way it inspires the masses by its revelation; if we are painters or sculptors we won't be producing landscapes or figures of

Mzwakhe Mbuli, people's poet: "Culture must be a weapon to raise the awareness of the people about their living conditions, the reasons for their suffering."

abstraction, but we shall and can paint portraits that symbolise important aspects of our liberation struggle.

The entire continent is soaked with blood,
The blood of gallant heroes of the soil.
Apartheid, the obstacle to peace and security
Shall come to an end.
The colonised society shall crush and grind colonial power
We shall double our assaults against evil
Ultimately there shall be peace and security

And the people shall govern.

▼
The Freedom Charter continues to stimulate cultural activity. This poster marks the 26th of June, Freedom Day.

XIV. The Freedom Charter and the working class

At the 1984 South African Allied Workers Union (Saawu) Congress, Curnick Ndlovu (centre) and Billy Nair (on his right), former Sactu leaders, share their experiences with the new generation of trade unionists. On their left is Sisa Njikelana, general secretary of Saawu.

29. In the workers' interest

The extent to which workers' demands are met in the Charter is a subject of considerable controversy. This section argues that the Charter primarily reflects working-class interests

There are people who question whether the Freedom Charter represents the interests of the working class. This doubt sometimes arises from a confusion between working-class demands that are also in the interests of other classes, and demands which are purely or primarily beneficial to workers.

While a demand for adequate education is in the interests of all classes, it is no less a workers' demand. Workers have an interest in peace. They have an interest in cultural development. They need freedom from arbitrary arrest. They need a house to live in and they need recreational facilities. In short, they have needs as workers and as human beings who have to exist outside the workplace.

While the Charter is not a programme of the working class alone, it nevertheless primarily reflects its interests. Some clauses of the Charter are socialist in orientation and are addressed much more profoundly to working-class interests than would be the case with any bourgeois document.

This worker orientation is attributable to the development of the labour struggle, especially in the 1940s and 1950s, and the part played by Sactu in collecting workers' demands. Two Sactu members, Ben Turok and Billy Nair, introduced and spoke to the clause of the Charter which reads "The people shall share in the country's wealth", a clause which clearly corresponds to workers' interests.

Many other aspects of the Charter are profoundly working-class in orientation. The clause "There shall be work and security" deals with such matters as the "right and duty of all to work". It also asserts the right to form trade unions, the abolition of child labour, compound labour, the 'tot' system and contract labour.

The clause entitled "There shall be houses, security and comfort" declares the right to decent housing and that slums should be demolished and unused housing space made available to the people. Rent and prices will be lowered. Instead of the present situation, where 'surplus' food is destroyed, the Charter declares that no one would be allowed to go hungry.

Some people, however, argue (we believe correctly) that the workers' interests lie primarily in the achievement of workers' control and socialism, but these critics say that neither is expressly mentioned. While this is true, the way that the clause on the country's wealth was introduced at the Congress of the People seemed to envisage that industries as a whole would be under the control of the people, that is the people's government. Under this general control, individual production units would be under the control of workers' committees.

Nevertheless, how this clause will be interpreted and whether or not the Charter itself will ultimately receive a socialist interpretation, will depend on whether working-class leadership is achieved and the extent to which the interests of other classes are transformed in the course of national liberation. Of considerable significance will be the extent to which the petit-bourgeoisie, intellectuals, workers on the land, the unemployed and other strata start to see their interests best fulfilled in an advance to socialism. This is not something that is achieved by words alone. It will depend on political struggle.

There is an analogy in the development and changing interpretation of the principle of self-determination in the United Nations. At the time of its creation in 1945 the United Nations Charter declared that respect for the principle of self-determination was of fundamental importance. Yet it simultaneously recognised colonialism. Indeed two of the leading United Nations members, France and the United Kingdom were, of course, in possession of large empires.

The treatment of self-determination in the United Nations Charter had been a product of compromise between states, at a time when the West was dominant in the United Nations, when there were few Socialist states in the United Nations and few independent African and Asian states.

Following successful national liberation struggles, the number of African and Asian states in the United Nations has continuously increased, thus strengthening the diplomatic power of these states, who often work in alliance with the Socialist states. In consequence, by 1960, a qualitatively different international relationship of forces had developed.

Even colonial powers came to recognise that colonialism was doomed (at least formally) and were compelled to recognise the principle of self-determination. Their conception of their own interests changed and consequently a new international consensus, considerably more radical than that of 1945, emerged. This was manifested, dramatically, in the 1960 Declaration, passed without dissent, holding that colonialism was illegal. Equally, in regard to apartheid, the international consensus has been dramatically modified. At the time of its inception, South Africa was a respected member of the United Nations. But apartheid is now treated as illegal and/or criminal, according to international law.

By analogy, if the democratic organisations struggling for the realisation of the Charter develop a working-class leadership and they convince themselves and other classes that there is a place for all under socialism, then it is likely that the democratic gains will deepen into socialism. It will be a deepening of both the national and the democratic character of the struggle.

Socialism is a democracy for the majority of the people, the working people, and instead of democratic rights being mainly formal, the material basis for realising rights are guaranteed. Under socialism, the national character of the state is also deepened in that the wealth, culture, all the assets of a particular state are more truly national assets, in that they are enjoyed by all. In a socialist state, 'the arts' are not the preserve of a wealthy elite. Equally, the culture of the people, in our case, that primarily of the African masses, would be regarded as belonging to all of us. Whites would see themselves as Africans and not Europeans.

Moreover, with socialism the national control over the economy against international imperialism will be advanced. At present, United States, British and other multinational companies take millions and millions of rands worth of profits out of South Africa. This is wealth made by South African workers. The fact that South Africa is, at present, so tied into the imperialist system, also means that the sicknesses of world capitalism (inflation and recession) get imported into South Africa. For these reasons the development of greater national self-determination and the development of socialism are closely linked together.

What we are saying, then, is that it is false to counterpose national liberation and socialism, for they are part of a single process. Realising the Freedom Charter is part of the struggle to achieve socialism.

We asked Billy Nair, veteran Sactu leader, about some of these questions.

Q: I'd like to pass on to another form of attack that seems to be coming from people who purport to be speaking from a socialist position. They say that the Freedom Charter is based on a multi-class alliance. They suggest that by catering for the aspirations of all these classes, we are not actually catering for workers' interests.

Now to what extent do you think that workers' interests have been found to be met in this kind of situation, and was there any alternative?

Nair: Well, the various clauses of the Charter, if you read it carefully, clearly show us that the basic interests of the workers are present throughout. For instance, the clause which says the "wealth of the country shall be restored to the people", the clause of the Charter dealing with the redistribution of the land, and that the people shall govern.

Right the way through you will see workers' interests represented, but not in isolation from other popular classes. Take for instance: "The people shall share in the country's wealth". That is fundamentally a working-class demand but the emphasis on the *people* is still relevant in that it shows the broad unity of all classes.

Now the orientation of the Charter itself is socialist, in that it is giving emphasis principally to the workers' demands. But at the same time it involves other sections of the community, be they the merchants, students, teachers etc. Hence the emphasis on the people. This is in order to broaden out the struggle, as it were. The alternative would be to drive those very classes into the hands of the ruling class.

Q: Do you think that a lot of these attacks that have come from purportedly left positions, are based on the assumption that working-class leadership means *exclusive* leadership, monopoly of that leadership?

Nair: Of course not. The workers, and the working class as such, did not regard itself as an exclusive club, isolating itself from the mass movement, the people's movement, but on the contrary, taking over leadership — not to the exclusion of other clases, but making its presence felt continuously.

Just to illustrate the point: Since the formation of Sactu in 1955, and even before that, the working class played a prominent role in the Congress movement, but more so since the formation of Sactu and of course you had leading members of the Communist Party earlier, playing a prominent role in the Congress movement as such. From the time of the formation of Sactu, Sactu cadres were actually politicised, educated, in fact trained to staff Congress branches in the first place. In Natal, in the Transvaal, you found Sactu cadres who rose from the ranks of the workers, rising to key positions in the provinces, and ultimately they rose to the national executive as well.

Natal is a good example, where you had people like Stephen Dlamini who is now secretary of Sactu, indeed Moses Mabhida, who is the general secretary of the Communist Party today. He rose from the ranks. He joined Sactu, rose to prominence in the provincial executive of the ANC, was then promoted to the national executive of the ANC. And we had many others, who rose from the ranks of Sactu and graduated up. So in that way, working class influence in the national movement was a predominant factor at the time of the banning of the ANC and that development is continuing to this day.

Q: Dominant within an alliance rather than exclusive leadership?

Nair: Ja.

Q: Could you be more precise. Why do we need working-class leadership? Is there some particular quality in the working class?

Nair: At times there is a romantic notion, on the part of some, that the worker is, *per se*, a revolutionary. On the contrary, a worker only becomes a revolutionary, in the classical sense or in the class sense, when he or she has imbibed revolutionary theory. Today we have, in Tucsa, a massive membership of nearly 500 000, or to put it correctly, I think it's about 486 000. But could you say that the organised group of workers in Tucsa are revolutionary?

Similarly, with those in other trade union federations, their mere organisation into a trade union federation does not *ipso facto* mean that they are revolutionary — they have to be armed with something more.

But to return to your question. What makes the working class so important is its objective position

Sarmcol workers on strike in Pietermaritzburg in 1985.

in production. Only the working class has the potential muscle to change our society. To do this, however, the working class needs allies.

Q: In 1955 would you say that workers were aware of all this?

Nair: The irony of the so-called workerist objections to the Charter is that it was the class conscious workers through Sactu and the trade union movement that preceded it, that were mostly responsible for the Charter. The greater the class consciousness of the worker, the more they see the need for a broader development of the struggle, for the formation of a broader united front against the ruling class.

The emphasis has always been to isolate the ruling class and not to strengthen its position. So any tactic that is employed by the working class that tends to drive segments of the black community into the hands of the ruling class would be suicidal.

Q: So you say the Charter then, although it's a popular document, nevertheless expresses workers' primacy, and that workers' interests are in fact guaranteed by securing the interests of these other classes, and not instead sacrificing them to the ruling bloc or ruling class.

Nair: Exactly, the dismantling of monopoly — if you hit the citadel of capitalism in this country, that is the smashing of monopoly, you would have gone a long way towards even destroying the very kernel of capitalism as such.[1]

Albertina Sisulu, president of the Federation of Transvaal Women and of the UDF, proudly demonstrates confidence in final victory — a victory ensured by men and women struggling shoulder to shoulder.

XV.
The Freedom Charter and women

30. Struggling shoulder to shoulder

Women, through the newly formed Federation of South African Women, were involved in the Congress of the People campaign. This section discusses the manner in which women's demands are raised in the Charter.

The first sentence of the first clause in the Freedom Charter demands that "Every man and woman shall have the right to vote for and stand as a candidate for all bodies which make the laws." From the start, then, the Freedom Charter links equality between women and men to its major political demand: "The people shall govern."

However, political equality is not good enough on its own. If women, one half of the people, are to take their rightful place, then they must be free of the special social oppression that affects them. This is not a concession to women, for without the fullest participation of women in the struggle South Africa as a whole will not be liberated.

In particular, the Freedom Charter voices the demands of the working women. The Charter demands equal pay for equal work for all, men and women. It demands creches and maternity leave on full pay for all working mothers. It demands free medical treatment with special care for mothers and young children.

In South Africa today 90 percent of single working women are also mothers. The demand for full maternity right is, in our situation, a radical working-class demand which women's organisations and the progressive trade unions are beginning to take up.

All other demands in the Charter, even when they do not refer specifically to women, have a particular importance for women. The demand for the land to be shared among those who work it, for instance, and the demand for an end to pass laws and bantustans, speak to millions of women trapped in rural poverty, trying to scratch a living from tiny plots of land.

In 1955 there was less emphasis than at present on the role of women in the struggle. This is reflected in the unequal participation of women in the collection of demands noted by several of those interviewed. It is also reflected in the relative weight of specifically women's demands in the Charter. There were, nevertheless, some outstanding women volunteers at the time. The newly formed Federation of South African Women (Fedsaw) played a significant role in formulating women's aspirations. *Women's Demands for the Freedom Charter* and a separate *Women's Charter* were produced by Fedsaw. (see below)

In turn, the impact of the Congress of the People campaign and the adoption of the Freedom Charter gave impetus to the women's struggle. This was to be carried to new and, as yet, still unequalled heights when in 1956, 60 000 women marched to the Union Buildings in Pretoria. It is significant that the original ideas for this march occurred at a Transvaal Fedsaw meeting to report back on the Congress of the People and the Freedom Charter. According to one informant, "We were looking for forms of action so we could begin to make the vision of the Charter a reality."

Francis Baard, founder member of the Federation of South African Women has seen the woman's struggle unfold for over 30 years. She was also a Sactu trade unionist and was banished in the sixties to Pretoria.

31. Carolus: "Things don't happen automatically"

Cheryl Carolus is an executive member of the United Women's Organisation (UWO) and former secretary of the UDF Western Cape. At present she is working in the UDF national office. In this interview she discusses her own background and how she sees the role of women in the Charter.

Q: Could you begin by telling us a bit about your background?

Carolus: Okay, ja, I was born in 1957. Since then I've been living in Silvertown. My parents had both grown up in Retreat. Then, just after they were married, their families were forced out; Retreat was declared a white Group Area. The families had to move in all together. I remember, in my childhood, we had my parents, my granny, her sister, my grandpa and four of us, the kids, in this self-same two-bedroomed house here in Silvertown.

My father was, still is, what is known as a printer's assistant. It's somebody who wipes off the ink and that sort of thing. A semi-skilled labourer. My mother used to be a nurse, but she became ill and stopped working when we were very young.

Q: Do you have memories of hard times?

Carolus: Ja. Quite a lot. Ja, I don't want to go into too much detail. The one problematic thing, and where probably I got a lot of my early politicisation, was my father's incredibly overdeveloped sense of justice. He was always standing up for some old *toppie*, say, whom the bosses had been messing around at work. He'd lose jobs because of standing up. That would mean hard times for all of us. Times when there was very little food in the house.

Q: And the women in your family?

Carolus: My mother is quite a strong person, not in the same vociferously articulate way as my father. More the kind of strength of having to cope with what I now (given a more sophisticated understanding) call the triple oppression of black women — oppressed by capitalism, oppressed by racism, and oppressed by sexism. She'd sit us down and explain what was happening. Always explaining the difficult situations to us — be it the fact that there wasn't food in the house, or explaining my father's feeling depressed.

Also, my mother has that attitude that you find in working-class communities like Silvertown. She always, always, to this day still, will give away her LAST. You share if somebody has got even less than what you have.

Q: When did you first get involved politically?

Carolus: I was quite young in fact. I was probably about 13 or 14 years old. At the time there was a big revival in the churches, the whole hippie era, everybody was singing songs about *Shalom* in the church. I got involved in the National Youth Movement, a 'multiracial' (as we would then call it) organisation, linked to the Young Christian Students.

In the same year, it must have been 1970 or '71, I bought my first political book — *Leila's Hijack War*. You know, Leila Khaled! I had this incredible romantic admiration for her, the picture with her Arab *doekie* and the machine gun... [laughing]. I think some people were very disturbed about it! I was in standard six then.

Any case, I joined up with the National Youth

Cheryl Carolus, executive member of the United Women's Organisation and a UDF official: "Every one of the ten clauses in the Freedom Charter, and not just a phrase here and there is also a women's demand, and has a special relevance to women."

153

Movement. In late 1972 us black students in the NYM started making contact with Saso [South African Students' Organisation]. There was a big debate whether we should form a separate black students' movement. We began to ask what role could whites play in the liberation of black people. It was a very traumatic thing. Lots of crying, and soul-searching, with militant agitation coming from the Saso ranks — these Afro guys attacking us, ja, for our 'white' values. The long and short of it, one fine day in the backyard of the Christian Institute we decided to split.

Looking back, I think the whole black consciousness experience was actually quite important. A lot of people who have their political roots in BC now speak disparagingly of it. But I think it was a particularly significant period of my life. I began to judge myself as a black person, not in terms of how I measured up to whites. At school we worked through the whole nail-polish, face complexion and lipstick thing — from a BC, not a feminist, perspective. We would say: "We are what we are, and we should be proud of it." Those kind of positive things were important, you know. BC was largely a cultural movement, that was its strength...and its limitation.

Anyway, under the impact of BC, at school (I was at Bridgetown Senior Secondary) we started organising a cultural society. Of course the emphasis was BLACK. There was just *no* other culture that was taken into account! A bit lopsided, nevertheless useful.

Somehow this whole thing got intertwined with religion as well. We had this bright idea that, no-o-o, we should actually look at Christ. We decided he was black. These whites had no right to claim Christ as theirs. We made a life-size painting of a *black Christ* on the cross, with enormous thick lips. We hung it up in the classroom. Our Afrikaans teacher, Mev. Boonzaaier from Bellville, thought it was *the* pits. It was bad enough that we'd already given her Langenhoven picture on the classroom notice-board an afro. And now, here was *this* blasphemy.

Q: Did the Unity Movement have any presence at your school?

Carolus: There were some teachers, but it was far too intellectual a movement, and it couldn't harness the militancy and anger we students felt. Also, Bridgetown was a mainly working-class school. Debating societies and such like didn't seem to equip us with the tools for understanding our oppression. I think the NEUM [Non-European Unity Movement], from their side, gave up on us as a bunch of peasants! Then I started at Bush (the University of the Western Cape) in 1976.

Q: Were you still very BC at the time?

Carolus: Ja. Absolutely, BC! I was detained in 1976, in my first year at Bush. I was inside from August to December.

Q: You were picked up for your part in...?

Carolus: Hmm, ja, now you sound like Majoor Louwrens of the security branch!

Well, getting back, even before I was detained some of us had an instinctive, gut feeling that BC was heading for a bit of a cul-de-sac. It doesn't mean we weren't impressed with the capacity of BC to *mobilise* people, that was its importance. But we saw that as its culmination, we had always said that BC is not an end in itself. We somehow felt we had to introduce more. We knew that people in Elsies River weren't just going to be rioting on the streets and then *boom* liberation would arrive.

So we decided to send a delegation to some of these Unity Movement people — at least to some who were then in that grouping. A number of students were officially, *nogal,* mandated dah-dah-dah to go and see the learned friends in the NEUM.

Well, the NEUM individuals were completely dismissive, which really, really made a lot of us fed up. They actually told the delegation to go back to their kindergarten and to sing their nursery rhymes....This was in '76 while the nation was burning, and we felt we needed a more scientific understanding to carry the whole struggle forward.

Q: Could you tell us briefly about the position of women in the BC ranks?

Carolus: BC was very *male*, women were just coincidental. Asserting your blackness went hand in hand with asserting your maleness. Just look at a lot of the language of BC, like the "emasculation of the Black people", I ask you. There was often very bad sexism, it was not just of the condescending, patronising kind. Many men in BC organisations felt they had to assert themselves over everybody, and more especially over the black women in the organisations.

Women were there, these chaps seemed to think, just to add a bit of spice to the black struggle. Women in the ranks were often harassed, and if you resisted, you were labelled 'bourgeois'. (You were either 'black' or 'bourgeois' — so much for the class understanding in BC!) Of course, there were some remarkable women, but they were few and far between. Nothing was done to develop women. If you developed in the BC ranks as a woman it was despite all the odds.

Any case, in '78, '79 I started looking at our history. Reading some earlier things, I started looking more closely at the Freedom Charter. But I wasn't adequately equipped at that stage to understand the Charter. It was only later in 1981 with the launch of the United Women's Organisation (UWO) when I became more involved in grassroots, organisational work amongst women, that the importance of the Freedom Charter became clearer for me.

While I had grown up in a working-class community, I had learnt most of my earlier politics in the student movement. The politics in my head and my own social background were not yet completely in step. Involved now with ordinary working-class people in an organisational context, I became more aware that the Freedom Charter wasn't just part of an heroic tradition, wasn't the expression of some worthy but empty ideals.

Millions of people in South Africa know they are oppressed, but they don't have the words to express that oppression. More seriously, for millions their oppression has come to seem like a natural fact, something unchangeable — you know, the south easter blows, so what can you do? The Freedom Charter spells out a different future, in very simple, but accessible terms. It is incredible to see the impact that these simple demands can have, when explained to people in the context of their daily struggles. The unimaginable becomes possible. It was only when I began working in the UWO that all this became clearer.

Q: But some people would argue that the Freedom

Charter hardly addresses women's issues at all.

Carolus: I think it's simply incorrect to say that women's problems are not catered for in the Charter. In the first place there are demands which relate explicitly to women. I think of the demand that "Men and women of all races shall receive equal pay for equal work." I think of the demand that "There shall be maternity leave on full pay for all working mothers." Then there's the demand that "Domestic workers" (who are mostly, though not all, women) "shall have the same rights as all others who work." There is the demand that "Free medical care and hospitalisation shall be provided for all, with special care for mothers and young children."

But every one of the ten clauses in the Freedom Charter, and not just a phrase here and there, is also a *women's* demand, and has a special relevance to women. Take the demand that pass laws must be abolished. It is women who are the most oppressed by the passes. It is mostly women who stand the first chance of being unemployed and endorsed out, who stand the last chance of getting a job; they are the people locked into the bantustans, forced to rear the kids, to till the fields. The demand that "Education shall be free, compulsory, universal and equal for all children" speaks meaningfully to women who are so often denied education because of their sex, as does the demand that, "All the cultural treasures of mankind" (MANkind???...ja well, even the Charter is not perfect) "shall be opened to all." How many women's horizons are limited by domestic drudgery?

Then, the demand that, "There shall be peace and friendship" has become a great deal more relevant in the 1980s than it was back in 1955. In this regard women play an important role in the whole militarisation of our society. While our men are forced to fight an unjust war, the system tries to build on particular values for women. They get women to believe they are homemakers, faithful and loyal wives to look after the children, and to knit socks for *pappie* and *boetie* on the border. It keeps the whole war psychology going. It would have been much more difficult if women had a different view of what their position in society should be. Even if women are not fighting, they can be upholding the whole militaristic system. But they're doing this in a different sort of way to the men. Which means *we* also have to address this problem.

Q: You mean we need to address women as women, and organise women into women's organisations?

Carolus: Yes. To an extent. But this relates mostly to the first and major demand of the Freedom Charter: "The people shall govern!" If women, one half of the people, are going to take up their rightful place in governing the country, then it is not good enough to piously talk of sexual equality. Things don't happen automatically.

We must never forget women in our society are not reared to become leaders, to be assertive. Instead they are expected to be submissive. In a women's organisation it is possible to give women that confidence and the necessary skills. You can give priority attention to it. It is simplistic to just leave this task to a civic organisation, say. Things tend not to happen that easily.

Look at some of our male comrades. They may treat me, after many hard, long, bitter battles, as an equal. That's fine, I'm a comrade. I have the confidence. I can shout, and probably swear as badly as they can too. But the way they treat their wives, their lovers, their sisters. It's such a contradiction! You'll go to somebody's house and you'll get introduced to all and sundry. But not the wife. Maybe they'll just very dismissively say: "This is my wife," not a person, just a 'wife'.

The problem is also more than one of attitudes. There are very practical, organisational questions. It is very difficult for women to participate in the struggle, because of the kind of roles they play at home. They work during the day, they come home, they must do the ironing, they must do the washing, the cooking, and see to the children. Then, if one looks at the number of meetings we have in organisations — now with UDF, heavens help us, we have a good few more meetings, like area committee meetings, regional meetings, GC's [General Councils], all thrown in for good measure. For a woman, whose children perhaps don't understand, it's extremely difficult to in fact participate like men.

One needs to look at the *times* we have our meetings. One needs to look at the *days* on which we have our meetings. One can't be idealistic saying that a woman should just put down her foot and leave the family, letting them starve. It doesn't happen like that. Ordinary working-class women have to come to terms with those things in themselves, and feel that they are not neglecting their families when they go off. Women's organisations have a special responsibility in all of this.

On the other hand, there mustn't be a wall between our different organisations and struggles. Here too, the Freedom Charter, by relating different demands together, plays a crucial role.

Sometimes in UWO we would get quite frustrated because we would build up women's branches, like in Macassar, and then we would, as we saw it, 'lose' many of the women to the civic. But after a while we said, no, it wasn't such a negative thing. Through an organisation like UWO we could build women to a point where they felt they could take their rightful place within a civic organisation.

We can't run around in concentric circles, if women's situation is going to improve, then we're talking about the whole societal system with *all* its values being changed quite radically. Women's liberation cannot be won in a vacuum. It has to be won side by side with other struggles. And this is where the Freedom Charter proves its worth. It draws together and relates a whole series of different struggles. The same system responsible for gutter education and poverty wages is responsible for the oppression of women. In daily work we must build in such a way that women take their full part in the national struggle to realise the ideals enshrined in the Freedom Charter.

32. Kwadi: Women's demands are the people's demands

Amanda Kwadi is an executive member of the Federation of Transvaal Women and holds the women's portfolio on the UDF Transvaal executive. The demands of the Charter, she says still speak for South African women.

To appreciate the type of demands made by women in South Africa, the context needs to be properly understood. We are waging a struggle different from that in the United States and Western Europe. Ours is for national liberation and the type of demands found in the Freedom Charter reflect this.

The vote is denied to black South Africans. That is so basic a right that it is taken for granted by Western European and United States feminists. Without the vote we do not control our own country, let alone have rights as women. That is why many of our demands are ones for which we struggle shoulder to shoulder with our menfolk.

Since the 1913 women's march to the Bloemfontein Administration Block against the Land Act, women have waged a number of campaigns. Growing maturity and consolidation led to the formation of the Federation of South African Women (Fedsaw) in 1954 and the adoption of its Women's Charter. In the forefront of this development were famous women's leaders like Lilian Ngoyi, Elizabeth Mafekeng, Albertina Sisulu and Helen Joseph.

Many of the demands of the Women's Charter

Amanda Kwadi, Fedtraw and UDF Transvaal executive member: "The struggle for women's emancipation in South Africa is inseparable from the struggle for national liberation, the struggle to realise the demands of the Freedom Charter."

and a separate document, The women's demands for the Freedom Charter, were ultimately incorporated in the Freedom Charter.

The demands of the Freedom Charter have not yet been met. Regarding the demand for "equal pay for equal work", women are *still* paid meagre wages and are *still* discriminated against at work. In a time of recession, such as we experience now, women are the first to be dismissed. "Full opportunity for employment" remains our demand.

"There shall be housing, security and comfort for all": Women all over South Africa are still staying in shacks, still squatting as is the case in Crossroads and Tsakane. Women and their families are still being forcibly removed from their home, as has happened recently at Magopa, Driefontein and KwaNgema.

"Rent and prices shall be lowered": Women are the ones who have to look after the children and maintain a household. They have to pay rents, feed the children and maintain the household. They are unable to do so because of the high rents and high prices. Evidence of this has been the rent protests involving women all over South Africa.

Women still demand "free medical services and hospitalisation". Maternity fees are very high. At Baragwanath one pays R45-00 a night. This amount is higher over the weekends and at night. Soweto women recently protested against this.

"Creches and social centres shall be built": Women are still demanding creches for their children. There are too few in most areas, and in some place, none. In Leandra and Soweto women built their own creches. In rural areas there are none.

The Freedom Charter calls for peace. Women had already endorsed this at their conference in 1954 when the Women's Charter was adopted. It stated: "We women of South Africa strive for permanent peace throughout the world". The demand for peace and friendship is more meaningful today, with the increasing militarisation of the apartheid state, than it was in 1955.

The struggle for women's emancipation in South Africa is inseparable from the struggle for national liberation, the struggle to realise the demands of the Freedom Charter. The Freedom Charter still lives today.

Long live the Freedom Charter!

33. Document: "The Women's Charter"

Adopted at the inaugural conference of the Federation of South African Women in April 1954, the Women's Charter stated the basic principles of the Federation.

PREAMBLE:

We, the women of South Africa, wives and mothers, working women and housewives hereby declare our aim of striving for the removal of all laws, regulations, conventions and customs that discriminate against us as women.

A SINGLE SOCIETY:

We do not form a society separate from men. There is only one society, and it is made up of both women and men. As women we share the problems and anxieties of our men, and join hands with them to remove social evils and obstacles to progress.

WOMEN'S LOT:

We women share with our menfolk the cares and anxieties imposed by poverty and its evils. As wives and mothers it falls upon us to make small wages stretch a long way. It is we who feel the cries of our children when they are hungry and sick.

It is our lot to keep and care for the homes that are too small, broken and dirty to be kept clean. We know the burden of looking after children and land when our husbands are away in the mines, on the farms, and in the towns earning our daily bread.

We know what it is to keep family life going in pondokkies and shanties, or in over-crowded one-room apartments. We know the bitterness of children taken to lawless ways, of daughters becoming unmarried mothers whilst still at school, of boys and girls growing up without education, training or jobs at a living wage.

POOR AND RICH:

These are the evils that need not exist. They exist because the society in which we live is divided into poor and rich, into black and white. They exist because there are privileges for the few, discrimination and harsh treatment for the many. We women have stood and will stand shoulder to shoulder with our menfolk in a common struggle against poverty, race and class discrimination.

NATIONAL LIBERATION:

As members of the National Liberatory movements and Trade Unions, in and through our various organisations, we march forward with our men in the struggle for liberation and the defence of the working people. We pledge ourselves to keep high the banner of equality, fraternity and liberty. As women there rests upon us also the burden of removing from our society all the social differences developed in past times between men and women, which have the effect of keeping our sex in a position of inferiority and subordination.

EQUALITY FOR WOMEN:

We resolve to struggle for the removal of laws and customs that deny African women the right to own, inherit or alienate property. We resolve to work for a change in the laws of marriage such as are found amongst our African, Malay and Indian people, which have the effect of placing wives in the position of legal subjection to husbands, and giving husbands the power to dispose of wives' property and earnings, and dictate to them in all matters affecting them and their children.

We recognise that the women are treated as minors by those marriage and property laws because of ancient and revered traditions and customs which had their origin in the antiquity of the people and no doubt served purposes of great value in bygone times.

There was a time in the African society when every woman reaching marriageable stage was assured of a husband, home, land and security.

Then husbands and wives with their children belonged to families and clans that supplied most of their material needs and were largely self-sufficient. Men and women were partners in a compact and closely integrated family unit.

WOMEN WHO LABOUR:

Those conditions have gone. The tribal and kinship society to which they belonged have been destroyed as a result of the loss of tribal land, migration of men away from the tribal home, the growth of towns and industries, and the rise of a great body of wage-earners on the farms and in the urban areas, who depend wholly or mainly on wages for a livelihood.

Thousands of women, are employed in factories, homes, offices, shops; on farms and in professions as nurses, teachers and the like. As unmarried women, widows or divorcees they have to fend for themselves often without assistance of a male relative. Many of them are responsible not only for their own livelihood but also for that of their children.

Large numbers of women are in fact the sole breadwinners and heads of their families.

FOREVER MINORS:

Nevertheless, the laws and practices derived from an earlier and different state of society are still applied to them. They are responsible for their own person and their children. Yet the law seeks to enforce upon them the status of a minor.

Not only are African, Coloured and Indian women denied political rights, but they are also in many parts of the Union denied the same status as men in such matters as the right to enter into contracts, to own and dispose of property, and to exercise guardianship over their children.

OBSTACLES TO PROGRESS:

The law has lagged behind the development of society; it no longer corresponds to the actual social and economic position of women. The law has become an obstacle to progress of the women, and therefore a brake on the whole of society.

This intolerable condition would not be allowed to continue were it not for the refusal of a large section of our menfolk to concede to us women the rights and privileges which they demand for themselves.

We shall teach the men that they cannot hope to liberate themselves from the evils of discrimination and prejudice as long as they fail to extend to women complete and unqualified equality in law and in practice.

NEED FOR EDUCATION:

We also recognise that large numbers of our womenfolk continue to be bound by traditional practices and conventions, and fail to realise that these have become obsolete and a brake on progress. It is our duty and privilege to enlist all women in our struggle for emancipation and to bring to them all realisation of the intimate relationship that exists between their status of inferiority as women and their inferior status to which their people are subjected by discriminatory laws and colour prejudices.

It is our intention to carry out a nation-wide programme of education that will bring home to all the men and women of all national groups the realisation that freedom cannot be won for any one section or for the people as a whole as long as we women are kept in bondage.

AN APPEAL:

We women appeal to all progressive organisations, to members of the great National Liberatory movements to the trade unions and working-class organisations, to the churches, educational and welfare organisations, to all progressive men and women who have the interests of the people at heart, to join with us in this great and noble endeavour.

OUR AIMS

We declare the following aims:

This organisation is formed for the purpose of uniting women in common action for the removal of all political, legal, economic and social disabilities. We shall strive for women to obtain:

(1) The right to vote and to be elected to all State bodies, without restriction or discrimination.

(2) The right to full opportunities for employment with equal pay and possibilities of promotion in all spheres of work.

(3) Equal rights with men in relation to property, marriage and children, and for the removal of all laws and customs that deny women such equal rights.

(4) For the removal of all laws that restrict free movement, that prevent or hinder the right of free association and activity in democratic organisations, and the right to participate in the work of these organisations.

(5) For the development of every child through free compulsory education for all; for the protection of mother and child through maternity homes, welfare clinics, creches and nursery schools, in countryside and town; through proper homes for all and through the provision of water, light, transport, sanitation, and other amenities of modern civilisation.

(6) To build and strengthen women's sections in the National Liberatory movements, the organisation of women in trade unions, and through the people's varied organisation.

(7) To cooperate with all other organisations that have similar aims in South Africa as well as throughout the world.

(8) To strive for permanent peace throughout the world.

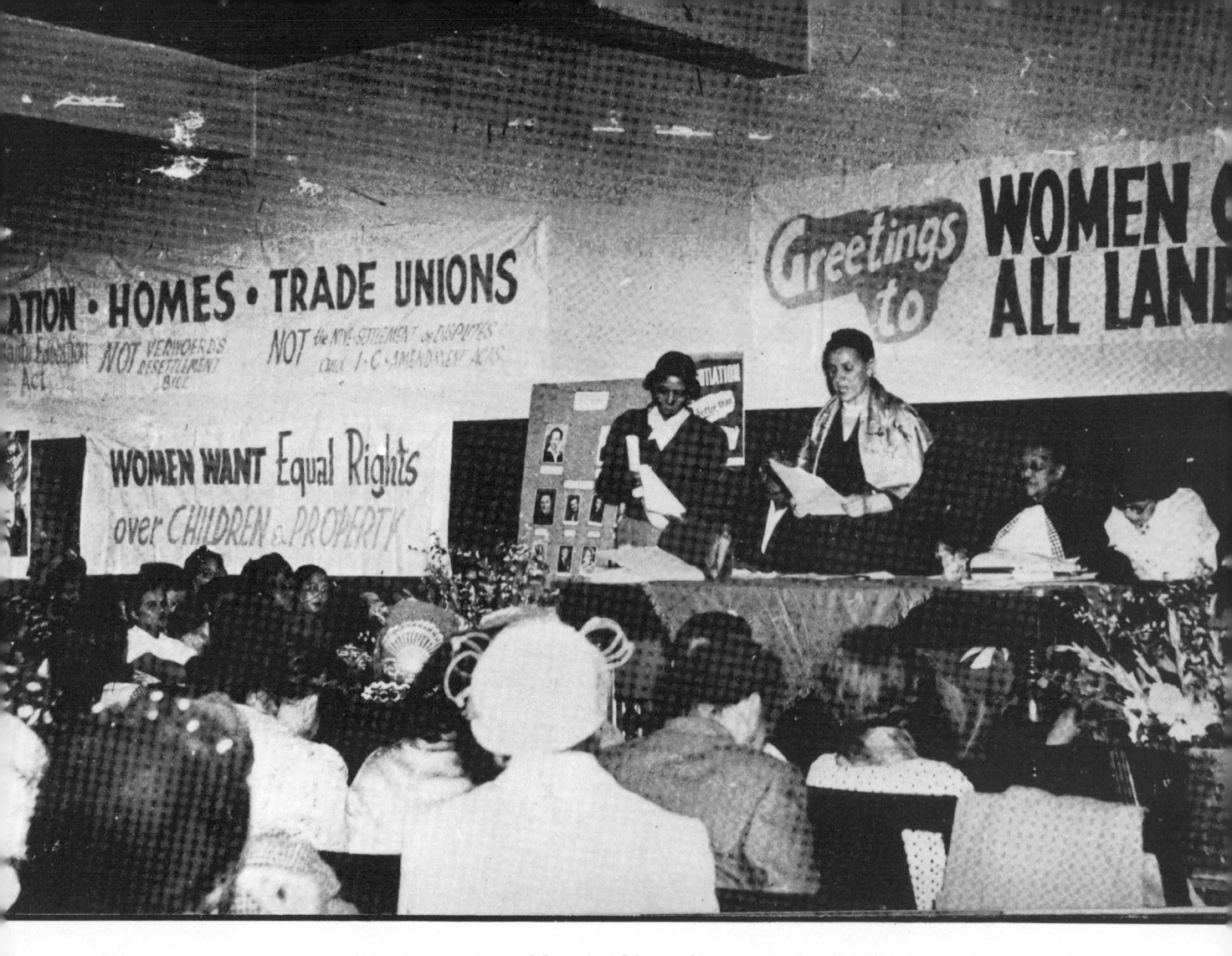

The founding congress of the Federation of South African Women in April 1954. It was here that the Women's Demands for the Freedom Charter was drawn up.

34. Document: "The women's demands for the Freedom Charter"

This document was compiled by the Federation of South African Women in preparation for the Congress of the People. Many of these demands found their way into the Freedom Charter in an abbreviated form.

WE DEMAND

Four months maternity leave on full pay for working mothers.
Properly staffed and equipped maternity homes, ante-natal clinics, and child welfare centres in all towns and villages, and in the reserves and rural areas.
Day nurseries for the children of working mothers.
Nursery schools for the pre-school children.
Birth control clinics.

WE DEMAND THESE FOR **ALL** MOTHERS OF ALL RACES.

WE DEMAND

Compulsory, free and universal education from the primary school to the University.
Adequate school feeding and free milk for all children in day nurseries, nursery schools, and primary and secondary schools.
Special schools for handicapped children.
Play centres and cultural centres for school children.
Properly equipped playgrounds and sportsfields.
Vocational training and apprenticeship facilities.

WE DEMAND THESE FOR **ALL** CHILDREN OF ALL RACES.

WE DEMAND

Proper houses at rents not more than 10 percent of the earnings of the head of the household.
Indoor sanitation, water supply and proper lighting in our homes.
The right to own our own homes and the land on which we build them.
The right to live where we choose.
Housing loan schemes at low rates of interest.
Lighting in our streets.
Properly made roads and storm water drainage.
Adequate public transport facilities.
Parks and recreation centres.
Sportsfields and swimming pools.
Public conveniences.

WE DEMAND THESE FOR **ALL** PEOPLE OF ALL RACES

WE DEMAND

Better shopping facilities, particularly in the non-European townships.
More dairies, and full supplies of pasteurised whole milk.
Mobile vegetable markets.
Subsidization of all protective foods: Bread, Meal, Meat, Milk, Vegetables and Fruit.
Controlled prices for all essential commodities: Food, Basic Clothing, Fuel.
Fair rationing of essential foods and fuel when in short supply.

WE DEMAND THESE FOR **ALL** PEOPLE IN ALL PLACES.

WE DEMAND

The right of ALL people to own and work their own farms.
The development of all uncultivated land.

The fair distribution of land amongst ALL people.
The mechanisation of methods of food production.
The scientific improvement of land by:
a. Irrigation and intensive farming.
b. Control of soil erosion and improvement of the soil.
c. Supply of seed to all people producing from the land.
Efficient organisation of the distribution and marketing of food.

WE DEMAND SUFFICIENT FOOD FOR **ALL** PEOPLE.

WE DEMAND

More and better land for the reserves.
Schools for children living in the reserves.
Maternity, medical and social services in the reserves.
Shops and controlled prices in the reserves.
Planned agricultural development of the reserves.
The abolition of migratory labour which destroys our family life by removing our husbands and which destroys their health through the conditions of their labour and the compound system.

WE DEMAND THAT THE RESERVES BECOME FOOD PRODUCING AREAS AND NOT RESERVOIRS OF CHEAP LABOUR.

WE DEMAND

The transfer of trust farms to the ownership of the African people.
The abolition of convict farm labour.
The payment of minimum cash wages for all men and women working on farms.
The abolition of child labour on the farms.
The abolition of the 'tot' system.

Free compulsory universal education for all children in rural areas.
Paid holidays for all farm workers.
The inclusion of farm workers in all industrial legislation.

WE DEMAND THESE RIGHTS FOR **ALL** PEOPLE IN THE RURAL AREAS.

WE DEMAND

That equal invalidity and old age pensions be paid for people of ALL races.
Homes and proper care for ALL aged and sick people.
National medical services for ALL sick people.
Adequate and equal hospital services for ALL people.
Increased cost of living allowances adequate to meet the rising cost of living.
That all African workers in all spheres of employment be covered by unemployment insurance and illness allowances.
The consolidation of part of the cost of living allowance into basic wages.
That no person be required to carry a pass or reference book.
Equal rights for ALL people.

WE DEMAND THESE FUNDAMENTAL RIGHTS FOR **ALL** PEOPLE.

WE DEMAND FOR **ALL** WOMEN IN SOUTH AFRICA

The right to vote.
The right to be elected to all State, Provincial or Municipal bodies.
Full opportunities for employment in all spheres of work.
Equal pay for equal work.
Equal rights with men in property, in marriage, and in the guardianship of our children.

AND TOGETHER WITH OTHER WOMEN ALL OVER THE WORLD

WE DEMAND

The banning of atomic and hydrogen bombs
The use of the atom for peaceful purposes and the betterment of the world
That there shall be NO MORE WAR
That there shall be PEACE AND FREEDOM FOR OUR CHILDREN.

"There shall be peace and freedom for our children," says the Women's Demands. Women in 1985 march on Moroka Police Station, Soweto to demand the withdrawal of troops from the townships.

"Knocking off", 5km from Oshoek where a resettlement camp was being built.

In the process of forced removals schools and homes are mercilessly destroyed. Here are the remnants of the school at Mahopa, destroyed by bulldozers.

Tshepo Khumbane, women's leader in the Northern Transvaal, describing conditions in the rural areas to the UDF first anniversary rally in Johannesburg, August 1984.

XVl.
The land question

35. The first demand in the rural areas was for land.

In the rural area land hunger was and still remains a major problem. Here we look at the importance of taking up this demand and organising in the rural areas.

While the re-emergence of mass democratic organisations in the 1980s has made a large contribution to the anti-apartheid struggle, these organisations have tended to be urban based. One of the most significant results of the Congress of the People campaign was to transform the Congress movement of the time into a truly national movement. While the Defiance Campaign had achieved this in the towns and cities, the Congress of the People campaign made the Congress Alliance into a mass movement in the rural areas. In Wilson Fanti's words: "By going out and talking to people the volunteers just put a light in the rural areas."

It is out of the Congress of the People campaign, conducted amongst workers on white farms, peasants on the land, migrant labourers on the mines and in industry, that the Freedom Charter demands concerning the land emerged.

To the contemporary democratic movement, many of the rural areas which previously boasted thriving ANC branches or sent delegates to the Congress of the People are unfortunately still unknown. To remedy this situation it is necessary to understand the specific problems that these people confront.

Thirty years after the creation of the Charter, we believe that the demands remain substantially similar.

It is true that since 1955 many hundreds of thousands of our people have become urbanised wage labourers. It is true that many hundreds of thousands living in the bantustans have no land whatsoever and think of themselves perhaps, not as landless peasants, but as unemployed workers, or as the families of migrant workers prevented by influx control from living with their bread-winners in the towns.

For many of these people the demand for the sharing of land, for seeds and tractors to be supplied by the government may not have relevance.

We would be making a grave error, however, if we underestimated the extent of land hunger still felt by many South Africans. Bantustan chiefs and government puppets continue to squeeze their own people. Absentee landlords continue to own vast tracts of land. Workers continue to produce wealth for huge agricultural enterprises while earning slave wages. Settled communities are violently removed from their ancestral lands and transferred to barren areas, losing what they have built.

To quote, Wilson Fanti, a leader of one such threatened community:

Fanti: So the first question [in 1955] was the land. Yes, that was the first demand [in the rural areas], which is *still* a problem today. ■

This view is confirmed by Dorothy Nyembe:

Nyembe: I remember, the people outside there [in the Natal rural areas] they wanted that they must get enough space.

Q: Enough land for themselves?
Nyembe: Yes. Even now they still want more land, more cattles. ■

The Freedom Charter's major demand concerning land is quite clear, all the land should be "redivided amongst those who work it, to banish famine and land hunger". The idea of 'sharing', or 'redividing' the land amongst those who work it in no way prejudges the issue of *how* this land is to be redistributed.

It is clear that the Freedom Charter seeks to abolish all racial restrictions on land ownership, and the idea of 'redivision' refers at least in part to this. Certainly the Freedom Charter does not set out to abolish all peasant farming. It explicitly says "The state shall help the peasants with implements, seeds, tractors and dams...."

The Freedom Charter, however, leaves open the question as to whether the bulk of the land will be shared out into small peasant plots, or whether it will be shared and worked *collectively* on a larger scale by an agrarian working class. Such matters will surely depend upon the degree of organisation, mobilisation and consciousness in the countryside.

To even *begin* to work in the rural areas we must develop a clearer understanding of the demands that are capable of mobilising the millions of people living in these areas.

Absentee landowners

All over South Africa there are farms owned by rich 'farmers' who hardly ever set foot on their property. Those who work the land live in poverty. Here Christmas Tinto tells a story about these farms.

Tinto: Recently I went to a farm at Durbanville

[near Cape Town], to my nephew who was sick there. I found them sitting there. I asked them: "Where's the boss who owns the farm?"

"No, he doesn't stay here. He comes here sometimes."

"What do you mean? Who stays there?"

"It's our coloured foreman there."

"Where does the boss stay?"

"He's in Port Elizabeth, coming here once a month."

"Who's doing the ploughing, and feeding this cattle?"

"We are," this African chap says. "We are doing the ploughing and harvesting of mealies and potatoes. We do."

They said: "Come here." I saw these stores of PACKED potatoes, hundreds of bags of potatoes. "What we do, we take these to the market in Goodwood. And the money, the boss comes and fetch it once a month. Ja, the man who is sitting in Port Elizabeth!"

I ask you now, whose farm *is* that really?

These huts in the Drakensberg have been marked as a prelude to the people's removal from their ancestral land.

XVII. The Freedom Charter and the petit-bourgeoisie

36. Our struggle is national

This section argues that the protection of small farmers, traders or manufacturers in the Freedom Charter is not a tactic or a trick. It is a commitment that flows from the nature of the South African struggle.

The rights of traders, small farmers and petty manufacturers are guaranteed in the Charter. This is not some tactical concession or an attempt to pull the wool over their eyes. This question must be considered from the perspective of both the struggle against national oppression and class exploitation.

The rights of these middle elements derive in the first place from the fact that our struggle is national. While the Charter is a document that primarily reflects working-class interests, it is nevertheless also a popular document, a programme for the liberation of all oppressed. The Charter demand that "the rights of the people shall be the same regardless of race, colour or sex", and the demand that "All people shall have equal rights to trade where they choose, to manufacture and to enter all trades, crafts and professions", speak meaningfully to the many thousands of black traders and shopkeepers. This stratum is nationally oppressed by Group Areas, and many other forms of racial discrimination.

At the same time, there is a class aspect to the question. These middle elements, and not just those among them who are black, are themselves in the thrall of the big monopolies who are squeezing them.

The clause relating to the nationalisation of

monopoly industry, banks and other financial institutions speaks not only to the interests of the workers, but is also aimed at all others who are dominated by the monopolies.

It is important to realise that with national liberation these middle classes and strata need not fear for their future. They would be allowed to pursue their occupations, subject to popular control.

Furthermore, it would not necessarily be incompatible with the interests of socialism to allow such strata and middle classes to continue to operate, subject to working-class control.

If a future socialist state were to take over the small enterprises in the townships, on the street corners, the barber shops, the small trades, the handicraft stalls and similar activities, it would undertake a huge burden. In order to manage the small enterprises it would have to establish a massive bureaucracy. Such activity might best be left in private hands, subject to state control. There are some types of work, like that of barbers, that are performed most efficiently on an independent basis. To nationalise them, as some states with a socialist orientation have discovered, may produce more problems than benefits.

The commitment to protect the rights of the petit-bourgeoisie is therefore not a tactic or a trick. It is a commitment that flows from the nature of the South African struggle and the continued protection of such rights, subject to controls, may be in the interests of both national liberation and socialism.

At the same time we do not wish to sweep under the carpet the fact that different allied classes and strata will also simultaneously have different, even contradictory interests.

The objective common interests at present, the struggle against national oppression and the struggle against the monopolies, does not cancel out objective particular interests of different classes. The commitment of different classes and strata to the common interest will vary in intensity according to the situation. The extent to which particular interests will be antagonistic or non-antagonistic with other classes will also vary.

We interviewed Billy Nair and Christmas Tinto on the question of the middle class.

Q: Now, what I'd like to know from you is whether you feel that these middle strata — the small peasant, the traders, even the small manufacturers whose rights are protected under the Charter, whether you feel their presence is in any way incompatible with national liberation and, secondly, with socialism. Can they exist under both types of social systems?

Nair: Oh yes. They'll continue to exist even after we transform our present society to the one we envisage under the Charter. We are not going at a wave of the Charter, as it were, with a waving of a magic wand to get rid of all that exists. We are going to have to carry over some of what exists in our present society into the new one.

In the course of this transition we are going to cater for small traders and small farmers, and to even protect them as long as they do not threaten to become big capitalists. Of course, the state would ensure that prices are strictly controlled, that they sell to state institutions, etc. In that way, growth of the small farmer into a big agricultural farmer, for instance, would be discouraged. What I visualise is the small farmer being given some means to pursue agriculture, as long as they do not threaten to become big landed aristocrats in the same way as today.

Q: I get the impression that some people in the democratic movement feel that we've got a secret agenda — that we aren't really serious when we say we're going to protect these middle elements' rights, and that they have very little to look forward to besides some day finding themselves against some wall. Do you think that such clauses in the Charter are merely a tactic?

Nair: Well, I think such thinking is actually infantile. It shows a complete lack of understanding of our objective conditions. In the first place, one of the bugbears of our economy today is the existence of monopolies in the industrial, mining and agricultural sectors. All classes, the working class, in particular, the small peasant, the small business people, even the small manufacturer, are caught in the vice-grip of the massive monopolies which have developed and which are being encouraged to develop by the Nationalist government.

Although they have the Anti-Monopolies Act and various laws to clamp down on the development of monopolies, actually the reverse has been taking place. So much so that today over 70 percent of the share capital of the entire stock market is controlled by six companies. There is increasing consolidation going on in the economy today.

Now the small man and woman in practically all sectors is hamstrung, and in fact is bound hand and foot to these monopolies. So this middle stratum is in its own way, waging a battle. Take the small boutiques. I read that in the Transvaal some of the whites who had developed small shops during the period of economic buoyancy have had to close. Because of strict credit conditions imposed by the banks, with which they were unable to comply, they had to fold up. Pathetic stories were published in the newspapers recently about their plight. So it is these small traders, hamstrung by monopolies, that we are seriously catering for. To suggest that we are merely using them for our own political aims is ridiculous. We are serious about this. We want to pit them against the real enemy, which is monopoly capital in this country. All is therefore grist to the mill in dismantling monopolies. In fact the clause relating to the nationalisation of monopoly industry, banks and other financial institutions is not merely in the interests of workers. It speaks very much to the needs of small business.

Tinto: We are pushing a wall of apartheid here. We have different ideas, but our immediate enemy in front of us is this apartheid. When this wall falls then we are going to say we know what else. There's a wall on the other side. But you can't reach that one now. We have got this immediate thing in front of us.

XVIII. The Freedom Charter and education

37. Opening the doors of learning

Students nationwide are calling for a non-racial democratic education. Their basic demands are similar to those made by students 30 years ago. Here we look at the educational clauses of the Freedom Charter.

At the time of the campaign to create the Freedom Charter, the Bantu education system had just been introduced. Volunteers were urged when campaigning for the Congress of the People to link the collection of demands to pressing grievances of the people, amongst others, that of Bantu education.

Since 1954 inferior systems of education, modelled on Bantu education, have also been introduced for coloureds and Indians. At the same time the content of white education continues to encourage racist attitudes and to discourage any sense of fellowship with black South Africans.

It is well known that the rejection of gutter education for a democratic educational system has now become a central arena of popular struggle. The apartheid government cannot meet the people's demands. The government's educational 'reforms' have been unequivocally rejected by the broad mass of students and parents. In fact, in the present economic recession the apartheid government does not even have the means to patch up gutter education sufficiently to continue its own limited 'reform' initiative.

In consequence of the continued rejection of this system, students have moved beyond protest. They have, more and more, advanced their own vision of a democratic, equal, non-racial educational system.

While such a vision is found in the Freedom Charter, the Charter's treatment of education is by no means comprehensive.

The Azanian Students Organisation (Azaso), Congress of South African Students (Cosas), National Education Union of South Africa (Neusa) and the National Union of South African Students (Nusas), democratic organisations affiliated to the UDF, have embarked on a project to create an Education Charter. This Charter does not seek to supplant the Freedom Charter. The Freedom Charter states basic principles and it makes particular demands. Some of these demands reflect the time when the Charter was written (though this is less true of education, than say Southern African affairs). To be more directly relevant to the field of education, the Education Charter could, if created through a sufficiently democratic process, establish what are the most pressing and specific educational demands of the 1980s.

It is likely once people have been widely consulted that new demands will be added to those found in the Freedom Charter. These demands would result on the one hand from the changes in the system of education, and the increasing state repression that is now a crucial component of that system. On the other hand, new demands would emerge from the increasing consolidation of popular, organised struggles against this education. This democratic student movement has thrown up new demands, most prominent being the demand for Student Representative Councils in schools.

Neither this demand, nor any other democratic demand, can be in conflict with the educational clauses of the Freedom Charter. The principles, though they may require elaboration, will remain the foundation of any Education Charter. It is therefore necessary to consider the educational demands of the Freedom Charter.

The educational clauses (which are linked to cultural demands) are headed "The doors of learning and culture shall be opened!".

This is the fundamental premise on which the new democratic people's education is based. No longer will education and access to cultural goods be the privilege of a section of our population, whether white or wealthy.

Racist rule has damaged the minds of both black and white. Courses in 'race studies', 'guidance' and even the more innocuous sounding subjects such as 'history' have filled the minds of whites with unscientific, poisonous, racist accounts of the place and contribution of blacks in this world.

White culture has been depicted as superior yet inaccessible to most blacks, especially Africans. Africans have been encouraged to 'develop along their own lines' with a frozen form of 'traditional culture'.

When the doors of learning and culture are opened, all will be able to realise their own talents. Education will be open to all and aimed at benefitting all.

The Charter declares that the "government shall discover, develop and encourage national talent for the enhancement of our cultural life".

At present 'national talent' means mainly whites and a few blacks who produce forms of art sufficiently insipid to be acceptable to the SABC and similar media. A democratic state would seek to encourage the talents of all South Africans, to provide the tools and skills that would make it possible for ordinary people, who may live in townships or far-away, little villages, to enrich their lives and thus to enhance South African cultural life in general.

"All the cultural treasures of mankind", the Freedom Charter continues, "shall be open to all, by free exchange of books, ideas and contact with other lands".

As far as the majority of South Africans are concerned, what they have access to, culturally, is mainly the decadent Dallas-type culture that extols values incompatible with the unifying, socially concerned and committed values of the Freedom Charter. Publishing and distribution is controlled by state and capital, to promote primarily racist values and/or profits. What is best in art, films and literature is, in consequence, scarcely available to most South Africans. In the cinemas in the townships and particularly on television, what is available is primarily low-grade car chases and glorifications of 'law and order' that contribute nothing to people's understanding of the world in which they live.

The Freedom Charter asserts that the "aim of education shall be to teach the youth to love their people and their culture, to honour human brotherhood, liberty and peace".

The injunction to "love their people" is in line with the preamble ,declaring that "South Africa belongs to all who live in it, black and white...." This is a direct attack on racism. It reaffirms the principles of a non-racial social order, where mutual respect and love supplant racism, hatred and suspicion.

The call to honour "human brotherhood" is fundamentally humanistic, that is, people are to be taught to care about their fellow human beings, as opposed to the racist doctrine of apartheid and the selfish, individualistic, dog-eats-dog morality of capitalism.

Liberty would be honoured because once achieved it needs to be continually safeguarded. Just as liberty is necessary to free education, peace is a pre-condition for the enjoyment of any and every freedom. While apartheid exists, there cannot be peace. When peace is established, it has to be defended.

Such education "shall be free, compulsory, universal and equal for all children". Economic factors can form no barrier. All people shall be able to attend.

Such education will be compulsory. This means that the state will be under an obligation to provide it. This is an obligation to end the cultural deprivation which has been the experience of all blacks, but especially Africans and workers. To provide skills and education to all is a condition necessary for the achievement of African and working-class leadership. Such education would be compulsory in another sense. Parents would not be able to shield their children from the democratic unifying principles of the new educational system. The attendance of children at school would be compulsory.

Such education would be universal, that is, its benefits would be extended to urban and rural areas. Arbitrary rules such as the present age limit for Bantu education, would obviously be abolished.

It would be equal education. There would be no

separate education, no private schools, no De Lange-type 'equality in own areas' reforms. It would be an education aimed at building a common national loyalty and culture.

"Higher education and technical training shall" under the Freedom Charter "be opened to all by means of state allowances and scholarships awarded on the basis of merit".

Instead of so much being spent on 'defence' (and here the demand for a democratic education links up with the struggle for peace, and the immediate demand to end conscription) and other repressive apparatuses, the new people's South Africa would be able to release funds to ensure that all have the opportunity to further their education to the highest level of competence.

The Freedom Charter is not only concerned with those who are already equipped to study. It also addresses the problem of widespread illiteracy. In some parts of South Africa, for example the Transkei, the rate of illiteracy has soared well above what it was in the last century. Illiteracy is an impediment to democracy and the participation of all our people in the control of their own lives. It needs to be wiped out with an urgent, massive programme, as has been implemented in socialist states.

"Teachers shall have all the rights of other citizens." This clause relates to their rights as salaried state employees and as citizens of a democratic state.

It will not be possible to arbitrarily reduce or subtract from teachers' salaries. Their participation in politics, far from being penalised, would be regarded as a right and a duty.

This education section of the Freedom Charter concludes by saying that the "colour bar in cultural life, in sport, and in education shall be abolished".

With regard to sport, the South Africa of the Freedom Charter would try to create healthy people, especially youths, with a broad interest in life. At present blacks have very limited opportunities to participate in sport. Playing fields are non-existent or in poor condition. Sporting equipment is beyond the means of most blacks and most black schools.

The abolition of the colour bar would, taken together with the Charter's broader egalitarian goals, ensure that sport would become a mass activity where all would be able to participate and maintain their health and enrich their recreational periods.

None of the principles or demands contained in these clauses need be supplanted by the Education Charter. Nevertheless, if the Education Charter campaign is conducted on similar lines to the Congress of the People campaign, if activists try to make it a national campaign, reaching and listening patiently to people in both urban and rural areas, it will be possible to supplement these clauses with more recent demands. In that way, by creating the Education Charter, our understanding of the Freedom Charter will be enriched.

The demand for democratic Student Representative Councils has been a key element in the struggle against Bantu Education in the 1980s.

38. Johnson: Four cuts for the Charter

Lulu Johnson, student leader describes the Freedom Charter's impact on his life.

Lulu Johnson first saw the Freedom Charter in 1981, when he was sixteen, during the school boycotts, when he got involved in Cosas.

Johnson: We were just having discussions and also reading some material at school, and when there were stay-aways in Port Elizabeth.

At that stage it was a matter of slogans. For example, we used "The people shall govern" intensively during the anti-Republic Day campaign.

I remember that I got detained for Section 22 and then, whilst I was inside, I had problems with the police. I was convicted with malicious damage to property for scratching, with a nail, the clauses of the Charter on the back of the door of my cell.

It was a matter of reciting the Charter clause by clause. Since then I have tried to understand it better. It's become clear to me that the Charter serves as an alternative programme. It shapes the future of our country in accordance with the nature of our national democratic struggle.

Q: Are the educational clauses of the Charter still relevant?

Johnson: "The doors of learning and culture shall be opened" is still our demand. We have the whole question of the age limit law and the payment of fees, money for books, school uniforms and so forth. This makes it impossible for many of our people to get education.

On the other hand, the Charter says that the doors of learning and culture shall be opened, irrespective of colour, age... and whether we have money or not these doors need to be opened.

Lulu Johnson, president of the Congress of South African Students at the time of its banning: " 'The doors of learning and culture shall be opened' is still our demand."

XIX.
"There shall be peace and friendship"

39. No peace under apartheid

The Freedom Charter might be 30 years old, but in many important ways it is as relevant, in some ways more relevant than ever before. This applies especially to its call for peace and friendship.

In 1955 the southern part of the African continent was not aflame with wars. Today large numbers of South African soldiers occupy Namibia and Angola. The apartheid regime has attacked, raided, coerced, threatened and destabilised all the states in the Southern African region.

In order to carry out these activities the South African regime has developed a large and sophisticated army and modern armaments industry. South Africa is widely acknowledged to be in possession of nuclear weapons. As a result of these developments, newly independent countries, desperately short of resources, have been forced to spend vast amounts on arms to defend their hard won independence. With this arms build-up on all sides, Southern Africa has become a powder-keg, a flashpoint. This is why the United Nations General Assembly has described the apartheid regime as a threat to international peace.

For its part, the apartheid regime says the instability arises from the alleged presence of ANC bases in neighbouring states. On these grounds the South African government tries to coerce its neighbours into so-called non-aggression pacts. It has rightly been said that peace cannot be achieved through such 'deals'. The flames of war that spread across South Africa's borders are the result of the situation within our country itself.

Peace must be made, in the first place, with the people of South Africa. That is only possible when the real source of aggression, the apartheid system, has been eradicated. To build the kind of South Africa envisaged in the Freedom Charter is to provide the conditions for achieving peace in our country.

In its preamble the Freedom Charter says "no government can justly claim authority unless it is based on the will of all the people" and that "our people have been robbed of their birthright to land, liberty *and peace* by a form of government founded on injustice and inequality" (our emphasis).

The preamble goes on to say "that only a democratic state, based on the will of all the people can secure to all their birthright that is, among other things peace without distinction of colour, race, sex or belief." To struggle for the realisation of the Freedom Charter is therefore to struggle for peace.

Racial oppression in our country has been built upon the violent dispossession and conquest of the indigenous Khoi, San and African peoples. In the case of the San, they were totally exterminated. The Union of South Africa could only be formed after the Boers and the British had defeated the long-standing military resistance of the various African peoples.

Through the Act of Union, the British handed over power to South African whites. Blacks were excluded from power and have since had to endure ever intensified racist oppression and class exploitation. Apartheid means institutionalised, permanent violence against South African blacks. It is this violence that has plunged our country into a state of civil war, and it is this violence that spills over our borders.

The violence of apartheid is manifested in a variety of forms including pass arrests and forced removals. The violence means tearing down plastic shelters and exposing people to the Cape winters, sending them to lives of misery, disease and death in bantustans: acts which might qualify as genocide under the United Nations Genocide Convention. [1]

The daily violence of apartheid breaks up homes, throws thousands of ordinary people into jail and exposes them to countless other indignities, injuries and humiliations.

Police intervention and violence is now an integral part of Bantu education and other education systems. It is nowadays as essential to the continued operation of gutter education that there be a police, and even an army presence, as it is to have teachers.

This poster was produced in the Vaal triangle shortly after the 3rd of September rising. The democratic movement maintains that apartheid means permanent war against the people of South Africa.

THERE SHALL BE PEACE AND FRIENDSHIP

C.
THE CHARTER TODAY

The Alexandra Youth Congress celebrate the 30th anniversary of the Freedom Charter.

XX.
Lekota: In search of the Charter

40. A personal account

'Terror' Mosiuoa Patrick Lekota at the time of going to print faces charges of High Treason. He has already served a term of imprisonment on Robben Island. This related to the period when he was a leading figure in the black consciousness movement. At present he is UDF national publicity secretary. He gives an account of his political evolution, leading to his support of the Freedom Charter.

In 1953 whilst travelling abroad Professor Z.K. Matthews was repeatedly asked by the many audiences that he addressed what type of South Africa the people of this country wanted in place of the present apartheid order. He was embarrassed by his inauthoritative replies to this question. Consequently, on his arrival back here, he raised the question within the African National Congress of which he was one of the leading members. This unchained a series of activities that led to the answer.

And so, thirty years ago the people of South Africa met at the historic Kliptown *pitso* (meeting place) and drew up the Freedom Charter as the programme of minimum demands for a non-racial and democratic future.

In search of the Charter

At the time of the great Kliptown come together the majority of the present generation of anti-apartheid activists were too young to make sense of that epoch-making event.

This unfortunate situation was worsened by the conscious attempts of the state to suppress the Freedom Charter and those organisations and individuals who were responsible for its drafting and popularisation.

The banning of the ANC in 1960, the arrest and imprisonment of its leaders, the banning and banishment of leading activists of that time, plus the exiling of uncompromising opponents of apartheid opened a wide and yawning gap between the following generations and those which had gone before.

But, as we shall soon see, this was only a temporary set-back. The youth of our country was determined to crown past efforts with success. And so, with uncertainty and painful slowness, black and white youth in the late sixties began to piece together the splinters from the repression waves of the early sixties.

The South African Students Organisation (Saso) emerged side by side with the National Union of South African Students and the University Christian Movement. With limited resources, on the one hand, and minimal information about our proud past on the other, we struggled to make the best out of a desperate situation.

We consoled ourselves, in the words of one speaker from those days, with the notion that in our struggle "we have a right to be right but, above all, we have a right to be wrong".

As the urgency of the South African political situation imposed itself on our youthful minds the second General Student Council of Saso conferred at the University of Natal (Black Section) in July 1971.

Leading black students attempted to define their vision of the future in what came to be the Saso Policy Manifesto. There were points of merit in the document no doubt, but it must be conceded that, looking back today, one can see gigantic oversights.

I think the same holds true for the Black People's Convention's (BPC) Mafeking Manifesto of 1975, even though the latter was a considerable improvement on the Saso Manifesto.

But we were also determined to discover our history. We knew that as long as we remained untutored in the history of struggle we would repeat the mistakes of the past. After all, it was obvious that the banning of the organisations and any literature on the struggle as seen through the eyes of the people was intended to keep us ignorant and easily controllable. For as long as our ignorance lasted the state and its agents did not show much concern. It contented itself with selective banning orders and periodic detentions here and there.

It was only when Saso and BPC celebrated Mozambican independence and, subsequently, after 1976 and all that went with it, that drastic action was forthcoming. While some were herded down to Robben Island, others lost their lives in incomprehensible circumstances while in detention.

A unique statement

It is not difficult to explain why these Saso and BPC essays and many other memoranda and manifestos are so hopelessly inferior to the Freedom Charter. The distinguishing feature is that intensive and extensive consultation with the masses of the people went into the drafting of the Freedom Charter. This singularly important feature is missing in the case of all the other documents — old and new.

I was part of the events of the period of the late sixties and early seventies and certainly we pursued our ideas with absolute honesty. At the same time, however, we were constantly aware that there were yawning and disturbing gaps in the solutions we proposed.

For instance, one of the major questions which we never could answer adequately was precisely what economic order we proposed. More specifically, how we would do away with the disparity in the distribution of wealth in our society.

In answer to these queries some hazy economic order called Black Communalism was proffered. The main features of this communalism were largely those of earlier African tribal society. But South Africa has advanced dramatically in the fields of technology, population, growth, education and culture, and the social structures of tribal society could not meet the organisational demands of our present highly developed country.

Even the idea of a 'ceiling' to the amount of wealth which an individual person could earn was impracticable. This involved a mechanical scheme whereby the maximum amount of wealth one could own was fixed say, for argument's sake, at R100 000. Anything beyond that could then be appropriated by the state and redistributed among the dispossessed or employed in the interests of broader society.

These ideas may have been honestly conceived and fervently pursued but they had serious flaws in practice. So, the search had to continue into our past. And in due course, those of us who continued to dig into the records of our oral and written history came across the Charter.

No sooner had we gone into its ten clauses than we acknowledged it as the most meaningful programme for a non-racial and democratic future. But others either did not discover the Charter or chose to disregard it. Again this is understandable, because the Charter is both simple and complex and some effort must be put into reading it. Those who adopted a negative attitude to this historic document continue to churn out manifesto after manifesto, as if our freedom will be speeded up by the rate at which we draw up memoranda.

Solves the people's problems

One has often been asked why and how one can come to accept the Freedom Charter as the most authoritative, comprehensive and acceptable statement for a democratic future. It is appropriate, therefore, that in this — the year of the 30th anniversary of the Charter — one gives as full a reply as is possible.

But first, let me state that the Charter is authoritative because the people were fully consulted as to its contents and everybody, including the Afrikaners, was invited to the People's Congress.

The Charter is comprehensive because it addresses every aspect of the problem of apartheid. It is acceptable because it embraces all the people of South Africa without discrimination on any basis.

Above all, however, the Charter addresses itself to the people's problems. To illustrate this point I wish to draw a little bit from my own background.

Restores the land to the people

The wars of dispossession (stretching from the late 17th century down to the Bambata rebellion of 1906), the Land Acts of 1913 and later, the Hertzog Acts of 1936, deprived African people throughout the country of whatever meaningful land ownership rights they had ever enjoyed. I have come to know what this means to us from my early years in the Free State.

My formative years were partly passed in the rural parts of that notorious province, more specifically on the maize farms of the Afrikaners. I use the word notorious advisedly, because I believe that of the provinces of South Africa the one which is most notorious for ill-treating African, Indian and coloured groups is the Free State.

I am confirmed in this notion by Sol Plaatje who has written that it was in that province where the most pernicious implementation of the 1913 Land Acts was pursued. The Free State Republic, like the Transvaal, never even so much as offered Africans the qualified franchise, which the Cape and Natal once offered.

It was in that province that pass laws were first extended to African women. For those of us whose roots lie there, the bitterness of the struggles of the Free State women resisters is the lullaby with which we were brought up. To this day the Free State is the only province in which Indian people may not settle at all, unless they change their identity in one way or the other.

As I grew up in those parts, I watched how year after year, my grandfathers, their neighbours and the whole clan ploughed, planted and reaped thousands of bags of mealies for their white masters. For their remuneration the farmer offered families an acre or two (depending on the fertility of the soil) to till for their sustenance. Such acres were chosen from the poorest part of the land and yielded the barest minimum of grain.

This practice of relegating our people to the parts of the land which are unproductive is the basis of white domination in this country. Whether on 'white' farms, or in the bantustans, millions of Africans are restricted to the poorest parts of the country.

The poverty in which the clan sweltered as a result of these conditions of life forced our people (as indeed it still does), to trudge barefootedly on icy-white frost. I remember how our feet cracked, how we developed frost-bite blisters. People took desperate steps to protect themselves, feet rolled thickly in sacking and stuck into crudely-contrived tyre sandals.

This is the reality of farmworkers' life in this country. The men and women who produce the sugar, grapes, watermelons, maize, wheat, beef, mutton are left with naught for their comfort. The labour force of this country's wine industry still receives a 'tot's' worth in wages. It is these conditions which the Charter addresses.

"Mayibuy' iAfrika"

The issue of land ownership rights has been at the heart of the struggle, especially of the African and Indian sectors and to a lesser extent, the so-called coloured grouping. Indeed, from the very beginnings of organised resistance right up to our day the slogan "Mayibuy' iAfrika" remains relevant. At the roots of this slogan is the painful realisation that only a tiny section of South Africa's people has access to land.

The call for the return of the land does not, as so many people misunderstand it, suggest the expropriation of white land and the expulsion of these white people. The point has long been conceded that even though white and Indian people originally came from other parts of the world, over the years they have become a permanent feature of the South African landscape.

We have all earned the right to live in this country by virtue of the respective contributions we have made in shaping it. As early as 1955 the people acknowledged this in the Freedom Charter. Even Saso later on asserted that South Africa is a country in which both black and white live and shall continue to live.

The central question, therefore, is how to restore land to the people of South Africa and redistribute it in such a way as not to prejudice any section of the population. We need a formula which will not deepen the alienation that is being generated by apartheid policies today. The Freedom Charter provides the most practical, fair and just approach.

"The land shall be shared among those who work it." Nothing could be more realistic. Any democratic South African, from whatever race or social background, will have an objective measuring rod. Does he or she work the land? Or is this person prepared to work the land?

This approach places land-starved and underpaid farm and rural workers in a position in which they will have fuller access to the land and enjoy the fruits of their labour. Where today a major portion of their labour is appropriated by the idle few, under the new order the greater portion of their work's produce will be enjoyed by the toilers and tillers themselves.

At the same time, by restoring the land to those who work it, the Charter simultaneously does away with the few who today own large tracts of land and do not work that land but fatten on the toil and tears of others.

This clause of the Charter returns land to Africans and the other underprivileged groups, without prejudicing the chances of whites to retain their own right of access to that land.

Above all, however, it also returns to the ownership of the people tens of thousands of hectares of South African land which is presently owned by foreigners. Many of these foreigners neither live in this country nor even know where this landed property is situated.

Lastly, it makes it possible for black and white South Africans to own land wherever they may choose. No longer will Africans be restricted to land ownership only in infertile, dry and overcrowded bantustan areas.

It is particularly this clause which initially, and continuously since then, convinced me of the significance of the People's Congress and the Charter itself. To my knowledge, no other document, produced by a representative group of people, has ever proposed such a practicable and objective measure as the solution to this aspect of the freedom of our country.

Work — the source of security

I have attempted to illustrate how I saw the Charter address practical problems of sections of our people in the bantustans, farms or rural areas. I must now turn to another clause that for me stands out in the Charter. But first the background.

At the end of the fifties my parents moved to Kroonstad where I joined them. Up until then both had worked in Johannesburg — my mother was a

Anglo-American workers on strike in 1981. "The Charter distinguishes itself as the only programme that carries hope for the millions of employed and unemployed workers in our country."

stay-in domestic and the old man lived in the backyard there under her cover. These things still happen today. As soon as I had moved to the urban areas, I realised how precarious life was there too.

Simply stated, one realised that the major effect of the systematic deprivation of Africans of land before and during the early part of this century, and the limitation of land ownership rights for the Indian and coloured section, reduced large portions of these groups to working-class status.

That is to say, for their survival our people have to rely entirely on gainful employment. And yet there were always those who were unemployed, whether retrenched, not allowed to work for lack of passes and related papers, or just unable to find work. This is outside of the fact of wages which were more often than not impossible to survive on.

I recall distinctly those suppers of porridge with black coffee when the old man was out of work. Sometimes it was just dry porridge. I remember families, less fortunate than mine, whose children ran the streets with buttock-less khaki pants. But worse, the many times when whole families, as in Crossroads today, had to spend cold winter nights exposed or under cover of bare plastic shacks.

I remember, too, conversations my parents and their peers had about the miseries of the squatters' struggles of the mid-forties in Johannesburg. How our people could not own land and therefore could not own houses. How the loss of a job led automatically to loss of a house. Endless stories of tragedies for one family or the other.

Often one would tire of eavesdropping on such gloomy stories, scamper away to join childhood friends on more exciting and fulfilling adventures — pilfering peaches or apples from the tree of a relatively hard-working neighbour. Children of the lowest stratum of the South African working class! We could hardly afford money for apples and food, which our own parents produced daily and in unbelievably large quantities.

That was in the early sixties. Around us, the marathon Treason Trial was drawing to a close, organisations were being banned and forced underground, in the case of the African National Congress, after fifty solid years· of non-violent campaigning. The defiant Nelson Mandela led his comrades into Robben Island Prison. The self-effacing Oliver Tambo ventured to set up the foundations of South African exile resistance politics. The Nationalists armed themselves with far-reaching measures such as 90-day detention and, later, the 180-day detention clause, for increased repression.

Less than a decade later, and now organised in Saso, we strained to understand the conditions of life of the black workers in the locations and in the townships. We followed them into the match-box houses of the townships, into the hostels, and the mine compounds. We considered their situation underground in the mine tunnels or high up on the top of ever-rising skyscrapers, on the vineyards and farms, in the bantustans. Everywhere we noticed, with a deep sense of indignation, that these workers had no security of employment or of housing — nothing whatsoever. Many of the unemployed were waylaying their more fortunate brothers and sisters, robbing them of their meagre wages.

At the time, without any trade union rights, they could not negotiate collectively for a living wage. As a result researchers uncovered wage-scales far below the national minimum level. This sickness of the pre-Wiehahn days is only just being addressed by the emerging independent unions. But even today, black workers still face summary dismissal if they go on strike — legal or illegal.

Black workers remain severely hampered in their fight for better working conditions. At least for the foreseeable future these constraints on their capacity to defend themselves will remain.

Insofar as the only guarantee for workers' survival, gainful employment, is sustained, and so long as our society is organised so that millions of workers remain unemployed there will be turmoil. Once more, I found the Freedom Charter to be the only document that adequately addresses this question. "There shall be work and security" — six words.

In enshrining the principle of work as an inviolable right of the individual in a new social order, the Charter at once eliminates unemployment and secures the jobs of those who are already employed. In this regard the Charter distinguishes itself as the only programme that carries hope for the millions of employed and unemployed workers in our country. Indeed, in providing security of employment, it automatically guarantees housing and food, because people who are able to earn a living wage can provide for themselves.

It is my firm opinion that, in the final analysis, what the workers want is not riches as such. What they want is the worth of their labour and a fair share of the wealth of their country. They want to be able to live like human beings and not like grovelling slaves. They are not in search of fantastic sums of money for which they have no practical use. They lack that poisonous yearning of some people to accumulate millions of rands with the sole purpose of decorating themselves.

What they want is the right to work, in conditions which are conducive to their health and for wages that will enable them to provide for their families. Effective trade union rights, as suggested in the Charter, will place the workers in a commanding position with regard to their terms of employment.

Uniting the people

I have set forth two clauses of the Charter which were a major influence in my attitude to that document. The other clauses of the Charter are not less important however. Throughout the Charter there is a strong yearning for the reconciliation of the people of South Africa. Perhaps the major worry of the present rulers of our country regarding the Charter is just this. Where their policies are divisive and alienating, the Charter reconciles and unites the people of South Africa.

But the Charter goes beyond our own country. It provides the basis for friendship and co-operation of the people of South Africa with those of neighbouring countries and beyond. It was a measure of foresight on the part of our forbears to have made a specific commitment to the maintenance of world peace. At the time of 1955 the daily menace of nuclear war had not yet become as threatening as it is today. The struggle for world peace is also a struggle in support of national liberation struggles. As long as sections of humanity remain under the yoke of imperialism, colonialism, oppression and exploitation the world will forever be a theatre of hunger, disease, turmoil and war.

It is these considerations which inspire our generation to say with those gathered at Kliptown 30 years ago: "These freedoms we will fight for, side by side, throughout our lives until we have won our liberty."

Curnick Ndlovu, executive chairperson of the UDF photographed in front of a banner containing the clauses of the Freedom Charter.

XXI.
Molefe: UDF and the Freedom Charter

41. Two documents — a single vision

Popo Molefe is the UDF general secretary. Like Lekota, he too has been charged with High Treason. He explains why there is no contradiction between the Freedom Charter and the UDF Declaration.

This year, 1985, will see virtually millions celebrate the 30th anniversary of the Freedom Charter. All democratic and peace-loving South Africans will demonstrate that the Charter still lives.

However, people are worried about the UDF marking the 30th anniversary of the Freedom Charter. They feel that the UDF has its Declaration and some people see this as a document that competes with the Freedom Charter.

I think that it was correct for the UDF to be launched without the formal adoption of the Charter. For historical reasons, some groupings might have resisted coming into the Front if we had been explicitly 'Charterist'. It was therefore correct not to insist on the adoption of the Freedom Charter. It is important to unite all democrats to advance the anti-apartheid struggle.

At the moment of the launch of the Front, such unity would not have been achieved on as wide a basis if the Freedom Charter had been adopted. It could not be a precondition for unity. Even today the adoption of the Charter might present a barrier against the incorporation of certain groupings. It might also lead to the disaffiliation of others.

When we speak of adopting the UDF Declaration

instead of the Freedom Charter we are talking of two documents that are at the same time different and similar. But don't forget, to subscribe to either is basically to subscribe to the same principles and to commit yourself to the building of a particular type of South Africa.

The Freedom Charter is a unique document, it was created by the people. It is not the vision of any one individual or group of individuals or any one organisation or group of organisations. It emerged, as this book shows, from the dreams and ideas of ordinary people. The Charter is authoritative because of this birth. It remains authoritative because it continues to reflect the demands of all classes of oppressed and democratic South Africans.

While the UDF Declaration also embraces these aspirations, it does not claim to be a people's document of the same sort. It is a people's document in the sense that it pledges people's organisations to come together to struggle against apartheid and for a democratic South Africa. But it was not, directly, created by the people.

It was drawn up by leaders of democratic organisations as a basis for co-operation between organisations. While the content of the Freedom Charter emerged from direct popular participation, the UDF Declaration, although it reflects popular aspirations, resulted from negotiations between organisations. The Declaration is the result of an agreement between organisations on the basis of their co-operation and the goals of their common effort.

Having outlined the difference in origins, one must note the very great similarity in their content.

The central thing about both documents is the demand that people must decide their own future in an undivided South Africa: "The people shall govern!" says the Freedom Charter. They must govern in the whole of South Africa, for South Africa "belongs to all who live in it, black and white, and...no government can justly claim authority unless it is based on the will of the people...."

The Declaration cherishes "the vision of a united democratic South Africa based on the will of the people...." The UDF stands for the creation of a democratic state "in which all South Africans will participate in the government of our country". Because it was written 28 years later the Declaration could also update the demand for a united South Africa by taking into account the bantustans:

"We stand for a single, non-racial, unfragmented South Africa, a South Africa free of bantustans and Group Areas."

Both documents refer to political, cultural and economic oppression under apartheid and both dedicate the people to struggle to eradicate these problems. The UDF Declaration makes reference to strategies and tactics to resist apartheid — in particular to resist the 1983 Constitution and Koornhof Bills. The Freedom Charter, in contrast, is a programme in the loose sense that it does not try to give guidance on how to proceed, what strategy and tactics are to be used to end apartheid. It is a programme in the sense of a vision of the South Africa of the future, the goal towards which we strive.

Basically, the goals of both documents are very similar. Both accept nothing less than the eradication of apartheid. They both dedicate the people to

From the Congress of the People to the launch of the United Democratic Front. One of the mothers of the South African liberation struggle, Helen Joseph, was present at both. Here she is speaking at the launch of the United Democratic Front.

struggle until a democratic people's South Africa is created.

The UDF has not formally adopted the Freedom Charter. Yet its vision of a democratic South Africa is the same vision as that of the Charter. There is no substantial difference. There is no reason why the UDF should not honour the document and play a part in its anniversary. In fact, as a front of people's organisations, the UDF has a duty to respect and honour landmarks in the people's history. One such landmark, in fact a crucial expression of our people, is the Freedom Charter.

XXII.
Tshwete: A People's Charter

42. Understanding the Charter clause by clause

Steve Tshwete is Border president of the UDF and former Robben Island political prisoner. He has been banished to the Ciskei, having been declared an 'undesirable alien' in South Africa. He provides a lively argument for the Charter's continued relevance.

The Freedom Charter belongs to the people of South Africa. Every one of the ten points in the Charter can be used to rally our people anywhere in South Africa. However the task of rallying our people requires that we understand the Charter for what it is. In this paper I consider some of the main features of the Charter and try to clarify what are, I think, misunderstandings about its nature. I then look at its major demands.

A People's Charter

The concept 'people' pervades the entire Freedom Charter. I want to argue that the Freedom Charter is not a class document, and that when you use the concept 'people' in the context of the national democratic struggle, you immediately usher us into an arena of class alliances, of class compromise.

All the existing classes and social groups (Christian, Moslems and intelligentsia) have been brought together for purposes of conducting the national democratic struggle. There is no question of playing one class against another. The emphasis is on national unity, and the immediate goal of all the classes and social groups in the alliance is the attainment of a popular people's republic in which they will have full participation.

The Freedom Charter will certainly usher in that sort of republic. It will not be a republic based on the dictatorship of the working class or the bourgeoisie. On the contrary, it will be a people's dictatorship. If I sound provocative on this point, I can only hope that I am sufficiently so. For it has been argued in the past, that the Charter is nothing else but a working-class, socialist document.

Among the champions of this school of thoughts are members of the Nationalist government. From this point of view in 1956, they tried to proscribe the Charter as a communist document, and the entire leadership of the Congress movement was put behind bars and prosecuted.

Whilst the government of this country has taken it upon itself to dub as communist all popular people's organisations, we should not lose sight of the fact that the Freedom Charter is not properly understood by a very large number of white people, particularly those still under the spell of the Nationalist Party. Hence the hysteria whenever the Freedom Charter is the issue.

There is another position that asserts quite vociferously that the Charter is simply a bourgeois declaration. It is argued that it is an anachronism of our time and bears no relevance to what they see today as a purely working-class revolution for the dictatorship of the proletariat. This is an ultra-left position which, of course, finds common ground with the ultra-right to distort and assault the freedoms enshrined in the Charter.

Both views seek to attach class connotations to the Charter. To my mind, this fallacy is generated by a lack of understanding of the history of the

Steve Tshwete, UDF Border president: "The Charter is no piecemeal social engineering. Given a chance to be implemented, the present system, based on injustices and inequality, must immediately give way." Here he is photographed at the Nusas July Festival in 1984 with Liz Abrahams on his right and Dorothy Nyembe on his left.

"The Freedom Charter is a condition for peace and friendship, not only inside South Africa which has been rendered a stranger to peace for over three centuries but also with our neighbours in Southern Africa." Here Steve Tshwete addresses the UDF launch in Cape Town in August 1983.

Charter. As long as we attempt to separate this document from its historical context and see it abstractly as the creation of a single mind, so long will we remain addicted to distortions and falsifications.

The Freedom Charter emerged at a very exciting period in the history of the national democratic struggle. The ANC, in particular, had matured into a broad mass movement, mobilising and uniting all sections of the oppressed and exploited, without any sense of discrimination in terms of class outlook. In that spirit, volunteers who were assigned the task of popularising the Congress of the People were not inspired by any class bias.

They visited factories, compounds, mines, churches, schools, universities, shops and business houses in the townships and elsewhere. They went to farmworkers and talked to peasants in the countryside. Religious, sports and other types of organisations were approached and asked to make their own demands.

I agree one hundred percent that the working class will always be the backbone of our struggle. And I agree that by reason of its overwhelming strength in the national democratic movement, there is bound to be a working-class bias all along the line of popular struggle. But in spite of it all, we must refuse to ascribe a class character to a document whose historical background shouts so loudly against such a position.

Reflecting reality

All people's programmes anywhere in the world spring from a given objective reality. Once it has been hatched the particular programme cannot be detached from its historical incubator. For the Charter was meant not only to project the ideal society, but also — and this is extremely important — to influence the situation in favour of the accomplishment of the ideal. If you take any programme from the Communist Manifesto of 1848 to the Freedom Charter, one eye will always be focussed on the present and the other on the future. The Freedom Charter, to be of any relevance, had to influence the objective reality in South Africa.

African Nationalism — the ideology of the national movement of the time — was the main mobilising vehicle. How could it, then, have produced a purely class programme?

Incidentally, at the time the ANC was also contacting other liberation movements in Africa which had, if any, very little sympathy with left-wing politics. Wouldn't a working-class programme have alienated our struggle from the rest of the continent? Certainly, that would have been sectarian and suicidal.

Again, the Charter had to influence the Western world and enhance the credibility of the popular struggle against the apartheid regime. This position would have been severely weakened had the people of South Africa come up with a document espousing the dictatorship of the proletariat. The socialist world and the people's republics in Eastern Europe would likewise have lost interest in our struggle if the Freedom Charter had turned out to be a purely bourgeois programme.

Except for imperialist and outright reactionaries, the Freedom Charter has been viewed by the entire progressive international community as the most ideal document to have emerged in this country. It has influenced not only the internal situation, but has played a significant part in its 30 years of existence in mobilising world opinion against the racist government. It is a charm of the United Nations.

Minimum and maximum demands

It is a document of minimum and maximum demands — maximum for the progressive bourgeoisie, a component element in the struggle, and minimum for the working class. In other words, the bourgeoisie will not strive for more than is contained in the Charter, while the working class will have sufficient cause to aspire beyond its demands.

What happens after the implementation of the people's charter — whether there is a socialist democracy or not — will certainly depend on the strength of the working class itself in the class alliance that we call a people's democracy.

If the working class is strong enough, then a transition to a working class democracy will be easily effected. At that point in time, there will be a realignment of forces. Mobilisation will be on a purely class basis and the working class ideology will constitute the engine of the transition.

But if, on the other hand, the working class has not been prepared for this historical role and is thus weak in the people's democracy, the bourgeoisie will turn the tables. There will be a relapse to pure capitalist relations of production. The Freedom Charter takes the working class a step nearer to its historical goal, whilst it does not tamper much with the bourgeois order.

"The people shall govern"

The Charter is no piecemeal social engineering. Given a chance to be implemented, the present system, based on injustice and inequality, must immediately give way. The type of government it envisages is a totally new democracy. "The people shall govern", it declares unequivocally.

The pertinent implication behind this assertion is that our country has never enjoyed a democracy in which all its people have equal rights and equal opportunities. The entire power structure is based on economic, political and social domination of the biggest majority. It is a mechanism of deprivation propped up by big capital to perpetuate the life-span of the ruling clique. Representation in the racist parliament in Cape Town is based on colour and property. The vast majority of our people have absolutely no say in the running of their country.

It is in this racist parliament that all the anti-people legislation is unleashed, and we have no way of protecting ourselves other than engaging in militant and popular resistance.

The Freedom Charter does not countenance this situation. It makes the point that every person black and white above the age of 18 years will have the right to vote for a candidate of his or her own choice, and be voted to parliament to represent his or her constituency without regard to colour, race or creed.

The present provincial and municipal administrations will not be left unscathed since they are ready gadgets at the service of the cliquist parliament to entrench racial and economic domination. These institutions, therefore, are anti-people and should naturally not see the light of day once the people start governing. They will be replaced by popular institutions geared to serve the interests and aspirations of the people as a whole.

The bantustans, management committees and all other puppet creations which have been imposed on our people to police, menace and maim them on behalf of the supermaster in Cape Town shall be dismantled forthwith. Every institution that carries some racial tag of any sort will be destroyed. All cliques shall have dissipated and the people's will shall bear sway.

"The wealth shall be restored"

"The wealth of the country, the heritage of all South Africans, shall be restored to the people." Monopoly industry and banks shall be nationalised to ensure that all our people have a share of the national cake. This is not the situation at present. Only a handful gormandises the fruits of the sweat and blood of millions of South Africans. Dockworkers toil at the harbours loading bales of wool to overseas markets and go home in the evening without even a decent coat to protect themselves against the elements.

This is the irony of life in racist South Africa, where capitalism has developed to the highest stage of monopoly. In such an economy, the position of the working class in particular becomes unenviable. It is a deplorable situation where just a couple of men are in control of the lives of millions of people. Workers can't escape the fatal grip of the monopolists. In the mines it is the same man. You run away and go to the textile industry only to meet the same man. He is running a big industrial empire under different names. Eventually his economic strength affects the political, social, spiritual and even the family lives of the vast toiling masses. He is not only the captain of industry. He has also become the captain of our destinies.

There can never be social justice in such a situation where exploitation is intense and pauperisation of the masses is sharp. The Freedom Charter sets us at ease here, particularly in its treatment of the national wealth. This clause pinpoints an injustice in the production and distribution of our wealth and offers to redress the situation.

"The land shall be shared"

The unfairness in the handling of the material resources of our rich country does not end here. In the countryside, one finds huge tracts of land in the hands of a small landed gentry. Some of them do not even stay at these farms except for certain evenings when they have a braai out in the country. They own large mansions and castles in the urban areas. They don't work on these farms, instead they employ white managers and enlist the services of African and coloured squatters. The squatters till the land and tend the stock of the 'groot baas' who may be basking somewhere in Mauritius. The laws of the country prevent the squatters from ever owning the land.

Again, the unfairness does not end with the squatters. There are villages dotting a large part of our country where the biggest outcry is land-hunger. These people have been given small pieces of land which is often barren and unproductive. The economy is barely subsistence. The best land in the country and the biggest slice of all land is, by legislation of the racist parliament, white-owned. Consequently these people die of starvation in the midst of plenty.

The Freedom Charter addresses itself to the plight of our rural people when it says: "The land shall be shared amongst those who work it." It shall not allow anybody to be in possession of huge farms and large mansions at one and the same time. As long as land is privately owned without the government having any say in the matter, so long will people starve and die. The present system of land tenure is a creation of the cliquist parliament and is therefore anti-people. It must be changed, so says the Freedom Charter.

"Houses, security and comfort"

Yes. The South African government and their supporters in big monopoly industry must be held responsible for deliberately leaving our people unhoused. They have never taken any interest in seeing to it that the millions suffering deep in the bowels of the earth, in industry and on the monopoly farms are accorded the status of human beings, provided with decent housing.

The ruling classes are not interested to know where and how the workers slept. All that matters is simply that these toiling men and women are back at work on time the following day to create wealth for them. How they came to work and how they went back to their 'homes' never bothered the ruling classes. There are slums throughout the country.

But the working class emerged from these situations and made its way to Kliptown, through police cordons, to demand houses. The demand still stands. They know that the South African government could house them if it were not devoting large sums of money to maintain a vast army of young men who are ordered to shoot to kill when workers make legitimate demands. The government is maintaining a huge well-equipped police force equally ready to shoot the hell out of the working class. Every year they buy new vans and hippos.

The people remain unhoused while the puppets, who are grease-boys of the machinery of oppression and exploitation, are decently housed. Look at the 'mayoral palaces' of the councillors and the large mansions of puppet presidents and ministers in the bantustans. Look at their BMWs and Mercedes Benzes sponsored by the big monopoly companies which amass huge profits by squeezing life out of millions of unhoused workers. In a democratic people's South Africa, there shall be houses because the people's government will be people-orientated.

What about "security and comfort"? We don't have them and we never had them. Pass raids at any hour of the day. The police have a licence to wake you up at midnight to demand a pass without any decency and privacy. There is absolutely no security and invariably no comfort. The Freedom Charter seeks to restore our human right to housing, security and comfort. It explicitly states passes shall be abolished forthwith and all identity documents will be the same for all South Africans.

Education and culture for all

From whatever angle you view apartheid, it remains the same thing — a statement of evil. When you are denied even such basic things as education and cultural development, then you start wondering why some people somewhere in the world still accord South Africa some measure of recognition.

"The ruling classes are not interested to know where and how the workers slept." This poster produced in the Western Cape during the campaign against forced removal to Khayelitsha, shows that workers *are* interested and demand "housing, security and comfort".

The Nats and their supporters have taken education as a weapon in their hands to maintain the relations of domination at all levels. They had to devise a system of education to de-educate the majority of the oppressed and exploited so as to maintain the myth of white superiority.

Verwoerd never minced his words when he piloted the Bantu Education Act at the very time when the great people of this country were preparing for the Congress of the People. In Verwoerd's words we were to be life-long hewers of wood and drawers of water. Bantu education would prepare blacks for the position of 'thatha-lapha ubeke-lapha' (doing unskilled work).

The present education crisis vindicates the relevant clause in the Freedom Charter, which completely destroys the myths of racist education as we see it today. The Charter says education shall be integrated, free and compulsory. It will be used as a means to advance the material and spiritual content of life in a country whose people shall have been re-united. The education of the child shall be the responsibility of the state. For how can one speak in terms of 'compulsory' education, as we often hear the bantustan captains say, when the entire expense of taking the child to school remains the task of the parent?

All national groups shall have equal rights

There is no reference here to the 'creation of four nations' — of whites, Africans, coloureds and Indians, as some detractors from the Charter would want us to believe. Firstly let us correct the silly notion of the 'creation' of nations. Some time back, I was told that Tshaka was engaged in a process of building a 'Zulu nation' when he was assassinated. I am not happy with this observation. I hold the view that building or creating a nation is not and cannot be the responsibility of an individual or several individuals. This approach sounds metaphysical and therefore unscientific and misleading. Yes, individuals can and do build bridges. But I am not convinced they can do the same with nations.

Nation building must be seen in terms of the economic forces at play. It is a historical process organised by forces other than individuals. Individuals merely become catalysts in an on-going process which they can delay but not stop.

I am impressed by the definition that a nation is a historically constituted group of people who stay within the same geographical boundaries, speak the same or similar languages, have the same or similar history, have the same or similar culture, have the same or similar psychological outlook, and who live under the same economic system.

But I am ill at ease with the notion: "Okay folks, let's build a nation along these or those lines." And a nation or four nations are forthwith supposedly created. The economic factor, to my mind, determines the constitution of various peoples into a single national entity. People merely promote or retard the process.

The most positive contribution of capitalism in South Africa, for instance, has been the complete destruction of tribal loyalties amongst the African people. There is no economic basis for the entrenchment of tribalism today. Without capitalism, the founding fathers' song in 1912: 'Zulu, Mxhosa, Msuthu manyanani' (Zulu, Xhosa, Sotho unite), would bear no meaning. It's the capitalist economy which made the slogan today's reality. And I want to believe that the process of integration has not been stopped with Africans of different tribal backgrounds, for instance. Under one economic system even broader integration can't be halted. Were it not for the reactionary legislation which hampers integration we could have been near accomplishment.

The Charter does not and cannot envisage any separate nations. All it did was to take cognisance of concrete factors in terms of which equality was and is distributed in terms of race and colour. It does not take a Utopian pose, that colour differences shall not be there. All it seeks to assert is that the colour of your skin shall not be used in any way against or for you in practically all aspects of life. We have to be realistic and always remember that we are not going to Icaria or some other Utopian island. The baby South Africa that is about to be born must, and will, bear the birthmarks of the cultural situation from which it emerges.

This phenomenon is universal and has been witnessed even in purely working-class revolutions. The Freedom Charter takes the position of a midwife who must have all the necessary gadgets for the safe delivery of the child, and who must also understand the delicate nature of removing certain unwanted things with which the child came out from the mother. To assume that the baby will be delivered neat and dry is to adopt the position of the most hopeless quack. The Charter steers clear of that stupidity. That is why it even goes to the extent of stating that the right of the people to "develop their own folk culture and customs shall be defended".

That is not in any way a suggestion of ethnicity.

No. For in South Africa nothing is going to disappear overnight — except apartheid. Certain people will still wear certain dresses and certain people will still demand *lobolo*[1] with all it entails for their daughters. All that is required is that your Afrikaans poems and Hindu dance and dress do not advance sectarianism and ethnicity because the Charter sees that as a crime against the people.

The material conditions will be such that all cultures will be developed towards the eventual emergence of a single South African culture. The Charter forbids the advancement of a culture that is incompatible with the progress of the people's democracy. Already one does observe the trend towards the miscegenation of cultures in South Africa, and such a process could have been long in advance in a democratic, non-racial setting where people mix freely, intermarry and go to the same schools.

Finally, it is not true to say that the Charter advances the 'creation' of any 'four nations'. On the contrary, it is a catalyst in the process of the emergence of a single, united, democratic people's South Africa.

Conclusion

Let us imagine a situation where residential areas are not allocated according to race and colour, where people attend the same schools, where all people have freedom of movement and association and can trade where they like, where delimitation of electoral constituencies is not determined according to race and colour, where there is no tricameral parliament and bantustans, where there is peace and friendship, where imprisonment shall be for serious crimes against the people and where all laws that smack of the slightest trace of racialism shall be abolished. It may sound quite idealistic when considered in the light of what is going on in South Africa today. But that is the firm message enshrined in the Freedom Charter. It is a condition for peace and friendship, not only inside South Africa which has been rendered strange to peace for over three centuries, but also with our neighbours in Southern Africa.

Once internal peace and security have been achieved, then the great people of South Africa will strive for international security and world peace. It will be a genuine undertaking not inspired by any sense of insecurity and fear as is the case with the men and women presently in Pretoria. Though we shall adopt the position of non-alignment, we shall nonetheless project the anti-imperialist attitude of the Charter.

May this document remain a source of inspiration till the dawn of that great day, which shall be given a name of those who shall see it. It shall be called the 'People's Day of South Africa'.

"The Freedom Charter provides a broad based progressive forum for those who are committed to self-determination for the majority of the people. Nothing could be more Christian than waging a struggle for freedom" — Father Mkatshwa.

XXIII. The Freedom Charter and religion

43. Mkatshwa: The Freedom Charter — a theological critique

Father Smangaliso Mkatshwa is general secretary of the South African Catholic Bishops Conference. He says all Christians committed to fighting for freedom should study the Charter.

What has the Freedom Charter to do with the Church today?

A lot! For one thing, many participants in the Congress of the People were professed Christians. For another, all progressive Christian Churches condemn apartheid as evil, heretical as well as theologically untenable. Modern theological scholarship is acutely aware that those who are committed to the struggle for total liberation must address themselves to the social, economic and political structures of the society in which they live.

The Freedom Charter provides a broad based progressive forum for those who are committed to self-determination for the majority of people. Nothing could be more Christian than waging a struggle for freedom.

At the theoretical or ideological level it is imperative for the Christian in South Africa to understand how apartheid serves the interests of monopoly capital and international imperialism. Through the Freedom Charter, thousands of people from all social classes and strata declared their option for a social order which would facilitate a fairer distribution of natural as well as other resources. They also wanted to create conditions

Father Smangaliso Mkatshwa, (centre) with Albertina Sisulu on his right and Dorothy Nyembe on his left, at the first anniversary rally of the UDF in Johannesburg.

where *"the people shall govern"*, where they will create and control their sovereign and independent countries. They committed themselves to a society wherein all *bona fide* South Africans would enjoy full rights of citizenship.

The Freedom Charter puts the human person right in the centre of the universe. It takes democracy quite seriously. That is why it is a people's document. The interests of the people are paramount.

Unlike the racially exclusivist 'national' convention of 1908-9, the Congress of the People was open to all those who subscribed to the values of a free, united, just and non-racial society. It is now generally acknowledged that the Congress of the People was the culmination of a struggle against white conquest, economic exploitation and political domination.

The historic assembly at Kliptown crowned its deliberations by producing the first anti-imperialist and anti-capitalist people's document in South Africa — the Freedom Charter. This document has continued to be the rallying point for all freedom-loving patriots who have an interest in the destruction of apartheid.

As we know, the Congress of the People was preceded by a series of intensive and candid consultations. On the practical level, the Charter can teach the Church much, even about itself. In the process of consulting, the freedom volunteers learned a lot from simple folks. They built up a formidable network of genuine communication and mutual respect between themselves and the people.

Finally, there is the unprecedented resurgence of interest in the Freedom Charter today. Apartheid, as a policy or political philosophy, is barren and discredited. People are searching for alternative models of society.

The Church cannot stand idly by if it wishes to promote the struggle for liberation and human dignity. Without any fear of contradiction it can be said that the Freedom Charter is compatible with Christianity.

The least that the Church can do, is to encourage its adherents to study the Freedom Charter and to enter into the debate surrounding the Charter, particularly during this 30th anniversary of its birth.

Not only is the Freedom Charter theologically sound, it forms a basis for a new society where all South Africans will have the right to be fully human.

44. Xundu: "I was present when the Charter was adopted"

Rev Mcebesi Xundu, UDF Natal chairperson attended the Congress of the People as a high school student. To this day he vividly remembers the joy and excitement when the Charter was adopted.

The Freedom Charter is the first document apart from the Bible which takes neighbourliness and loving your brothers and sisters in the community seriously. Its unbanning is good news for Christians.

I was present when the Charter was adopted on June 26, 1955. When we met in Kliptown, I was in Std 9 at St John's College in Umtata. I belonged to the ANC Youth League, and attended the Congress as a member.

Before that, I had attended a few Youth League rallies, but the excitement we experienced at Kliptown was something I had never known before.

It was exciting because people were declaring openly that political rights could be available to all, regardless of age, colour, sex, wealth or education.

It was also the first time that we tried to solve our problems on a non-racial basis.

After discussions were held, and the Charter was drawn up, it was read out to everybody. The joy that was there was as if a baby had just been born.

Because of its fundamental Christianity, the Charter still has tremendous potential for change in South Africa. The document will be criticised by black consciousness bodies and other groups who want short cuts.

To fight for a democratic future, through democratic methods, is much harder and people will often try to short-circuit what is difficult. The Charter lays down the value of disciplined democracy.

Father Albert Nolan: "Since the Churches are called to read the signs of our times, the Freedom Charter should be taken seriously as one of the signs of our times, and as one of the places we must look to for the prophetic voice of God."

45. Nolan: The Freedom Charter and the Christian Churches

Father Albert Nolan is a Catholic priest and former head of the Dominican order Southern Africa. The Freedom Charter, he says, is one of the places where we must look for the prophetic voice of God.

Unfortunately, in most of the Christian Churches in South Africa, the subject of the Freedom Charter is approached with a certain amount of fear and trepidation. This is not so much because of the contents of this famous Charter; rather it is the result of many years of government propaganda. Until recently it was not altogether clear whether the Freedom Charter as such was banned or not. This has tended to make some people, including some Christians, fearful of reading it or possessing a copy. It has also led some people to think that the Charter must be a very radical and dangerous document, especially when it is associated with the ANC which is portrayed as a 'terrorist' organisation.

Anyone who does take the trouble to read the Charter, against the background of all the unfavourable propaganda, must surely find it surprisingly moderate and obviously just in its demands. Any Christian who reads it must surely find it perfectly in keeping with the demands of the gospel. During this year, the 30th anniversary of the Charter, and now that it is clearly not banned, there can no longer be any excuse for the Churches not reading it and commenting on it.

From the point of view of Christian faith then,

what can one say about the Freedom Charter?

Although the Charter was finally formulated as a list of demands, the grievances of the people behind these demands are clear and unambiguous. We have heard these grievances again and again since 1955, but here in the Charter we have the voice, not of this or that organisation, but the voice of the majority of the people. From the point of view of Christian faith this is the cry of the poor and oppressed, that even today is being heard by God himself. God can say today, as he said long ago of the Hebrew slaves in Egypt: " I have heard their appeal to be free of their slave-drivers...the cry of the sons of Israel has come to me and I have witnessed the way in which the Egyptians oppress them" [Ex 3:7,9]. It is like the cry of the oppressed widows and orphans that God has promised to listen to [Ex 22:22] or the cry of the labourers whose wages have been kept back: "Realise that the cries of the reapers have reached the ears of the Lord of hosts" [James 5:4].

If God himself hears the cries of the people expressed in the Freedom Charter, then surely the Churches too must listen, must take heed and must act upon it. In these circumstances there is no other way of remaining faithful to the God of the Bible.

But what about the specific demands made by the people in the Freedom Charter?

Criticism is cheap. It has often been said of the Churches that they criticise so much, so easily and yet they seldom make any suggestions about a viable alternative. It is, of course, true that the proposing of alternatives is not the business of the Church; but here is an alternative, here is an alternative proposed by the people themselves. The role of the Church in these circumstances is to comment on the proposed alternative from the point of view of God's justice.

It may well be that the Freedom Charter as a blueprint for the future is defective. Perhaps the economic and social implications require further elaboration and perhaps the political and ideological implications of being anti-capitalist without being clearly socialist require further study. But this is not the concern of the Church as Church. The document of the Church will be concerned with the *values* embodied in this Charter. Are they the values of the gospel, the values of God's kingdom or not?

What is needed is a careful comparison between the values expressed in the Freedom Charter and the values expressed in the Bible, or in the social teaching of the Churches that is based upon the Bible. For Catholics this social teaching is set forth most authoritatively in the social encyclicals of the Popes. Making this comparison I myself can find no contradiction whatsoever between the Freedom Charter and the Christian social teaching.

The Charter calls for an end to discrimination: "All laws which discriminate on grounds of race, colour or belief shall be repealed." It calls for equal status and equal opportunity for all the people of South Africa "regardless of race, colour or sex". Equality is one of the most cherished values in the Bible. We are all made in the image and likeness of God, and the Church has always preached respect for the human dignity of every human being.

Much of the Charter is an appeal for basic human rights: the right to vote, the right to education, housing and work , the right to form trade unions, to travel freely, to worship, to receive medical care and so forth. There is in theory no difference between the rights demanded here and the statements of the Churches about human rights.

The Charter also demands that the wealth and the land be shared by all, for the "well being" of all. Sharing is a basic Christian value that finds expression in the equal distribution of the promised land of Canaan [Numbers 33:50-54; Joshua 13:21], in the tradition of almsgiving and of selling one's possessions to share the proceeds with the poor [Mt 6:19-21; Lk 12:33-34; 14:33], and most of all in the first Christian community that shared everything [Acts 2:44-46; 4:34; 5:11]. The manner in which this sharing is organised politically and economically is not spelt out in the Charter nor in the Bible. Whether it involves some form of socialism or not makes no difference to the all-importance of the value of sharing itself.

In no way does the Freedom Charter call for violence. In fact it emphasises that "peace and friendship amongst all our people shall be secured by upholding the equal rights, opportunities and status of all". What is foreseen is a South Africa that "shall strive to maintain world peace and the settlement of all international disputes by negotiation — not war".

In brief, the Charter is simply an appeal for true democracy in South Africa: "The people shall govern...because South Africa belongs to all who live in it, black and white." There is a mighty expression of hope here, a hope that a Christian can only describe as prophetic.

I would therefore dare to say that, since the Churches are called to read the signs of our times, the Freedom Charter with all its possible limitations be taken seriously as one of the signs of our times, and as one of the places we must look to for the prophetic voice of God. The Freedom Charter can help us to bring our abstract principles and statements down to earth. And even more importantly it can challenge us to look more critically at our real motives and assumptions. Maybe God wishes to make use of the Freedom Charter this year.

46. Kearney: "... and owned everything in common."

Paddy Kearney, director of Diakonia in Durban, finds many parallels between the Charter and the Bible. Here he looks at the principle of sharing land and wealth.

Is the Freedom Charter still relevant today, 30 years after its first publication? I am convinced that it is, and that the vision of society which it proposes is the only sure way to achieve a genuine and lasting peace in South Africa.

As a Christian I have been struck by the similarity of the Charter's message to that of a much older document — the Bible. Like the sacred writings of Hindus and Muslims the central message of the Bible is that all human beings are made in the image of their creator — God. Because human persons are made in God's image they enjoy an infinite dignity. All should therefore be accorded an equal dignity, rights, opportunities, an equal share in wealth, land, education and decision-making.

I would like to look at just two of these — the sharing of land and wealth — to show how the ideas of the Freedom Charter have close parallels in the Bible.

In the Old Testament a remarkably radical idea is proposed — the 'Jubilee Year'. It was prescribed that every 50th year, all land was to be returned to its original owners, without compensation, and all debts were to be suspended or cancelled. So the land was to be equally divided, and those who had accumulated vast tracts, found themselves having to part with these. It is significant that what was called for was not a hand-out from the rich to the poor, but a radical redistribution, that is, justice.

We are not sure how often or how extensively the prescription of the Jubilee Year was carried out in Old Testament times, but in the New Testament we see a similar idea carried out even more frequently by the early Christian community. So we read, in the 'Acts of the Apostles'.

"The faithful all lived together, and owned everything in common; they sold their goods and possessions and shared out the proceeds among themselves according to what each one needed....they shared their food gladly and generously." [Acts 2:44,45,47]

"None of their members was ever in want, as all those who owned land or houses would sell them, and bring the money from them to present it to the apostles; it was then presented to any members who might be in need." [Acts 4:32-35]

Many more parallels could be drawn between the message of the Bible and that of the Freedom Charter, but I hope these will be enough to show how foolish is the view that the Charter is 'Moscow inspired'.

The vision of a new society put before us in the Freedom Charter — like that proposed in the Bible — has obviously not yet been achieved. The 30th anniversary of the Charter's publication is, however, an opportunity to redouble our efforts to ensure that it is implemented.

Youth celebrate the 30th anniversary of the Charter in a church. "As a Christian I have been struck by the similarity of the Charter's message to that of a much older document — the Bible."

231

47. Tutu and Naude: Our common humanity

Bishop Desmond Tutu, former general secretary of the South African Council of Churches (SACC) and 1984 Nobel Peace Prize winner and Rev Beyers Naude, present SACC general secretary see the Charter as a document which would bring about peace in South Africa.

Rev Beyers Naude

In the Christian tradition, Churches throughout the centuries have shared with many other groups and communities a concern for justice. This concern also includes constitutions of countries and charters defining the basic rights of individuals and communities. The Freedom Charter is an example of such an expression of the people. I believe that the time is overdue for all Churches in South Africa to embark on as in-depth a theological analysis and evaluation of the Charter as it deserves, being a document which has a clearly expressed concern for justice, freedom and full participation for all people of our land.

Bishop Desmond Tutu

Many say we have entered a period of reform which will gather a momentum of its own and go beyond the intentions of those who set it in train. Those who say this, point especially to the fact of a new constitution as evidence of this change.

Others have equally vehemently denied that we are in a reforming era, pointing especially to the same constitution as evidence of the determination of the ruling minority to retain power in the hands of the very few whilst assiduously excluding the vast majority of South Africans. They point to the fact that this new constitution was produced by a small but dominant section of our society and unilaterally determined.

Isn't it remarkable that our fragmented and deeply polarised society did once produce a document which bore the stamp of popular approval because it was truly and yet incredibly a document produced by the people.

I refer here to the Freedom Charter which is the handiwork of South Africans of all races and colours and ages, who gathered in Kliptown in 1955. It spoke about our common humanity and our common South African citizenship. It spoke about a sharing society, about a caring community, about a compassionate fellowship. It spoke about providing for each according to their need and deriving from each according to their ability. It spoke about a just, participatory and sustainable society. It spoke about a human society because it described a humane society.

It gloried in our interdependence for that is how God intended us to live, it is the law of our being and when we contravene it then all kinds of things go wrong. Then we have endemic unrest. Then we abrogate the rule of law, then we resort to detention without trial, to arbitrary bannings, to teargas, police dogs and bullets and to the army being quartered on a peaceful civilian population. We resort to violence.

How I pray that we would tear up all the constitutions we have, and sit at the conference table (all the authentic representatives of every section of our society) and work out a blueprint, black and white together, of a new society truly just, democratic and non-racial. And the Freedom Charter could provide a valuable foundation document.

God wants us all, black and white together, to walk tall as we stride together, black and white together, hand in hand into the glorious future which He is unfolding before us all, black and white together.

Rev Frank Chikane: "If you read the scriptures from the perspective of liberation and of justice then you see the Charter."

48. Chikane: "It depends on where you 'key in'"

Rev Frank Chikane is a former member of the UDF Transvaal and national executive and vice president of the Soweto Civic Association. Presently he is facing charges of Treason. He is also the director of the Institute for Contextual Theology. He came across the Charter when he was involved in the black consciousness movement but did not see the two as contradictory. Here he explains why.

Q: How did you discover the Freedom Charter?

Chikane: When I came to university there were reading materials available and I began to read about the history of the fifties and before. I began to read books by Mandela and so on which were floating around. That's when I came in contact with the Freedom Charter. My immediate reaction was: "I mean this document is so good! It's so Christian!" For me as a Christian I just found it a fantastic document.

The non-racial stance just made so much sense to me. Then, I didn't see it as a contradiction to the BC [Black Consciousness] approach at all. I just saw it as expressing the reality of the type of society we wanted to have.

Q: Were you involved in the BC movement at University?

Chikane: Ja, when I came to Turfloop it was automatic to become a member of Saso [South African Students' Organisation]. The organisation was seen as an internal mobilising force which didn't necessarily take a particular position vis-a-vis the exiled organisations. So, at that particular moment we saw BC as a way of making blacks to be conscious and accept themselves as human beings.

We never saw it as an end in itself. In my opinion it was a means to an end.

Q: To what end?

Chikane: The end is that we'd move into a non-racial type of society where there would be justice. You use BC for people who still want to get out of that depressed state of accepting that they are less than human. Immediately they have got out of that, they are able to focus on a more concrete desirable society that we intend to look into.

Q: So you are saying that there's no barrier between BC and a non-racial position? That it is not necessary to counterpose the two?

Chikane: Ja, I think you can't actually put one against the other. I think it is a stage of development of any black person who has been oppressed for a long time.

For example, when we started the UDF, we had house meetings. In Diepkloof, an innocent old person asked: "But you have a 'Boraine'[1] on your executive, how does he come in?" It's not that that person is reactionary. It's only because of the reality of his conditions, that he asks that type of question. It's natural. One has to go through a certain development to be able to understand society better and reinterpret it in a different light completely.

Q: When we say we are in the democratic movement, this doesn't mean we're opposed to BC?

Chikane: No, no, no.

Q: I think some people feel we've got to oppose it whereas you are saying it is part of a process?

Chikane: Yes, it's part of a process. As you are confronted by various issues, you develop and reach a level of understanding of society, of the type of struggle we are fighting and what we want to achieve out of that struggle. Only when somebody takes BC as an end in itself, then we get into problems. That person doesn't see anything beyond just BC.

It is those organisations that have actually tried to identify BC with an anti-position to the Charter, that have caused the problem.

What I have realised is that the people who shoot the Charter, shoot it for different reasons rather than the Charter itself. People find themselves making certain alliances which are seen to be not within the fold of the Charter. Then this makes them look for something to attack in the Charter.

I feel most of the criticisms have been quite unfair. Let me quote an old man in the African Independent Churches who said: "You can't change the Charter. The people who drew it, some of them are dead already and they expressed their feelings. We should value the document as it is." The critics are interpreting it in the light of their experiences in a particular context.

Q: As a Christian, do you feel that there are any problems about Christians supporting the Charter?

Chikane: I don't think there is any problem because the Church is based on a just system. The pattern when you read the Charter is that of producing justice, producing peace. The words 'justice' and 'peace' actually signify the Kingdom of God and if the Church is working towards the Kingdom of God, then the Charter becomes a document that is very relevant to that type of Kingdom of God.

Q: Some people feel that some parts of the Charter reflect an ungodly atheism. For instance the section: "The people shall share in the national wealth." They worry that there's something unchristian about this.

Chikane: Well, if you are a victim of Western propaganda then you are bound to see a lot of atheism in the Charter. But if you are not indoctrinated and you look at the Biblical tradition critically then you realise that *that* is actually what the tradition is talking about: that we have to be a sharing community.

The Bible even goes as far as talking about selling property and redistribution. Paul says you shouldn't feel you are burdened when you are required to share with your brethren so that there can be equality. The impression is given that some will have, so that others should not be in need. So, if I have the potential ability to produce more, then I am doing it for those who are not able to do so. Therefore I become of service to other people.

If you read the scriptures from the perspective of liberation and of justice then you see the Charter. If you read it from the perspective of the oppressor and the dominant classes, then you are bound to see communism instead of justice.

Q: So you say there are two ways of reading the Bible?

Chikane: Ja, in fact, radical biblical scholars have come to accept the Bible as a document which is a reflection of class conflict. It depends on where you 'key in'. If you key in from the side of the oppressor then you see the texts and concepts and symbols that represent your perception of life. And if you view the Bible from the point of view of the oppressed you actually see God in action on the side of the oppressed classes. You'll have the dominant against the weak and the word of God keeps coming back on the side of the weak, the orphan, the crippled. And you see Jesus associating himself with the least of the people in society; the 'rabble' as they called them.

Q: Do you think the Charter is still relevant — you know it is 30 years old now. Do you think it still speaks to the needs of ordinary South Africans?

Chikane: Having been involved in the study of a document as old as the Bible, one actually appreciates reading a document like the Charter. As a historical document it is quite inspiring.

It reflects the feelings of the people during that time. The Charter doesn't use high flown jargon of scholars. It uses the ordinary language of the people expressing their grievances. And I'm saying that the very demands they were making, are still the demands today.

"The land belongs to all who live in it." We can still repeat it today. That's realistic. That's fair. That's just. That's Christian.

You know, "The people shall govern." I mean, the people *must* govern. You can't have somebody governing people who are not participating in the government. We don't have that.

I don't see anything in the Charter that is incompatible with the reality that we are facing at the present moment.

49. Buthelezi: There is nothing unchristian about the Charter

Bishop Manas Buthelezi, president of the South African Council of Churches, argues that the Charter would create a valuable framework for preaching the gospel.

Buthelezi: As a Christian, I think that when it comes to blueprints — whether it's a political blueprint, economic blueprint — the important thing is to ask whether that particular blueprint serves the purpose of enriching the lives of the people and how they relate to one another.

Will the document or blueprint enable people to live harmoniously together and improve race relations which is an issue in our country? Will it serve as an alternative to the blueprint of the unacceptable policy of separate development? These are some of the criteria in reading the document. There is nothing in it that is inconsistent with the Christian faith. Of course it is not a Christian document and doesn't claim to be one. But that's not the issue. The issue is that when you talk about how to run the economy of the country there is nothing unchristian about it.

Q: Some people say the clause "The people shall share in the country's wealth" represents an atheistic doctrine?

Buthelezi: No, that's not a problem from a Christian standpoint. It's rather from an economic standpoint. Some people subscribe to certain economic principles regarding how to structure the economy of the country. There is nothing Christian about that — whether you opt for socialism or capitalism. The question is whether the chosen system provides an equitable sharing of wealth.

Q: Sharing — is there a Biblical basis for that?

Buthelezi: Sharing is a Biblical principle. God's gifts must be distributed amongst God's children: "The land shall be shared amongst those who work it." Of course there is nothing inconsistent with the Christian faith in that. Far from being that, it's what we preach. If you work you must enjoy the fruits of your work.

"All shall be equal before the law" speaks for itself. We are all brothers and sisters in Christ.

"There shall be work and security." Yes, we have a Christian ethic of work. It's Christian to work.

Q: Do you feel that the Charter furthers the preaching of the gospel?

Buthelezi: We believe that in order to promote what we understand to be Christian love, it's necessary to have a framework — to have structures which do not choke the expression of Christian love. The present political structures are not consistent with the preaching — with the promotion of the preaching of the Christian gospel. Far from being that, they throttle the preaching of the gospel.

The Charter is a blueprint on the basis of which healthy political, economic and social structures will be built. I would say it would create a very important framework and atmosphere for the preaching of the gospel. Where there is no justice the work of the Church suffers. People should have a share in the wealth of the country — otherwise we will fight over its division and peace will suffer.

Bishop Manas Buthelezi: "Where there is no justice the work of the Church suffers.

50. Langeveld: A challenge to the Church

Father Chris Langeveld is the parish priest of Phiri, Soweto. The Church has for too long looked at history from the top instead of from the bottom, from the perspective of those who suffer. To do this the Church should take note of the Charter, he says.

Langeveld: The Freedom Charter, for me, is a very big challenge to the Church. Here we have the most democratic and most widely canvassed expression of what the people really feel about their situation. It is not only a denunciation of what exists but it announces a project for their liberation in their own language expressing their own interests.

The Church, together with the dominant forces in society, has for a long time looked at history from the top, in other words, from the position of people with privilege and power. Now, I think, is the time to look at history from the bottom, from the perspective of those who suffer under that system.

This is not to say that the Church has sided with the people at the top but rather the perspective the people have had of the Church has largely been from the top. Even when the Church has made good statements on behalf of those who are struggling against their oppression, it has always been *on behalf of* the people and now is the time for the Church to speak *with* the people.

What do I mean when I say 'speak with'? You see, 80 percent of the Christian Church in South Africa is made up of people who come from the exploited and oppressed masses. Therefore that voice should carry a lot more weight in the Church and their experience should be reflected in its structure and functioning.

When people come to Church on Sundays they come with their experience of oppression, they come with their language, their race, they come with their memories of struggle. How has the Church accepted that reality? How has the Church interpreted and allowed the people to interpret their faith and their practice of faith in the light of their experience? I think very little has been done. But there have been very good signs recently that the Church is more open to allowing this experience to challenge them.

The Church has made a lot of pronouncements about the injustice of the apartheid state. Many of these pronouncements are very good and contribute significantly towards cutting off the lines of retreat of the state. By that I mean the state has for a long time tried to rob Christian symbols and theology of their subversive significance and they've tried to press that theology and understanding into the service of the project of the privileged.

I think the Freedom Charter contains in very earthy, blood, sweat and tears, the actual aspirations of people and it expresses their plan to become liberated.

Because the Freedom Charter is such a democratic document and because it allows the oppressed and exploited to speak in their own language the Church has an obligation to take that seriously. We have to change the situation where the pronouncements of the Church have come largely from the privileged sectors of the Church and thus are framed in the language of those sectors. Even if they speak on behalf of those who suffer, they are not using their language.

The Church has to move one step further and listen to what the people are saying about their own conditions, analyse and assess it and include what they are saying in their whole denunciation of apartheid.

Q: Is there anything in the Freedom Charter that you think speaks specifically to Christians?

Langeveld: Actually, I think every single clause speaks to Christians.

If you look at the clauses, they compare very well with the understanding of the 'Kingdom of God' that Christians have. The symbol of the Kingdom of God is a symbol that captures the aspirations of people for total liberation. Many of the clauses are giving concrete expression — giving flesh — to the real aspirations of people in South Africa. In that sense they approximate to the total liberation spoken of in the Kingdom of God symbol.

You can take any one clause and see how compatible it is with biblical Christian teaching.

Let me take the clause "There shall be peace and friendship". Christians often claim that they are called to love, called to be peacemakers. That's exactly what the Freedom Charter is saying in this clause. Until there is a democratic, independent unitary state in South Africa, we cannot be at peace with one another. In fact, the apartheid system in South Africa puts people in conflict with one another. The racist apartheid regime declares war on the majority of the people. So we're living in a state of war.

What the Freedom Charter is saying is that we need to change these conditions so that there will not be structural war between people anymore. I think that's a profoundly Christian ideal. It expresses what Christ meant in the Sermon on the Mount when he says "Blessed are the Peace Makers". Through the Charter, the peacemaker is active; the Freedom Charter is not keeping the state of peace, but is working towards making the conditions for peace. The Freedom Charter is saying that — that we need to establish the conditions for peace in South Africa. And that means that apartheid, racial capitalism has to go.

If you take the whole prophetic tradition of the Bible, we see that there's always a concern for the outcasts or the orphans or the widows. And this was said in the Freedom Charter: that *all* should have houses, security and comfort.

In the clause "The doors of learning and culture shall be opened" you see the universal understanding of the Kingdom of God — that there's no race, no people that can be excluded from God's Kingdom. Racial apartheid by definition is exclusive. And that's at odds with the whole Christian message of universalism.

Q: What avenues are there in the Church for promoting the Charter?

Langeveld: Firstly, in the educational sphere the Church immediately runs into a whole range of contradictions. It has to teach in racially segregated schools which goes against the ethos of Christians. When they struggle against this racial separation they need to reflect on the clause of the Freedom Charter that "The doors of learning and culture shall be opened".

In their hospitals and clinics the Church needs to reflect on why it is that they are being forced to

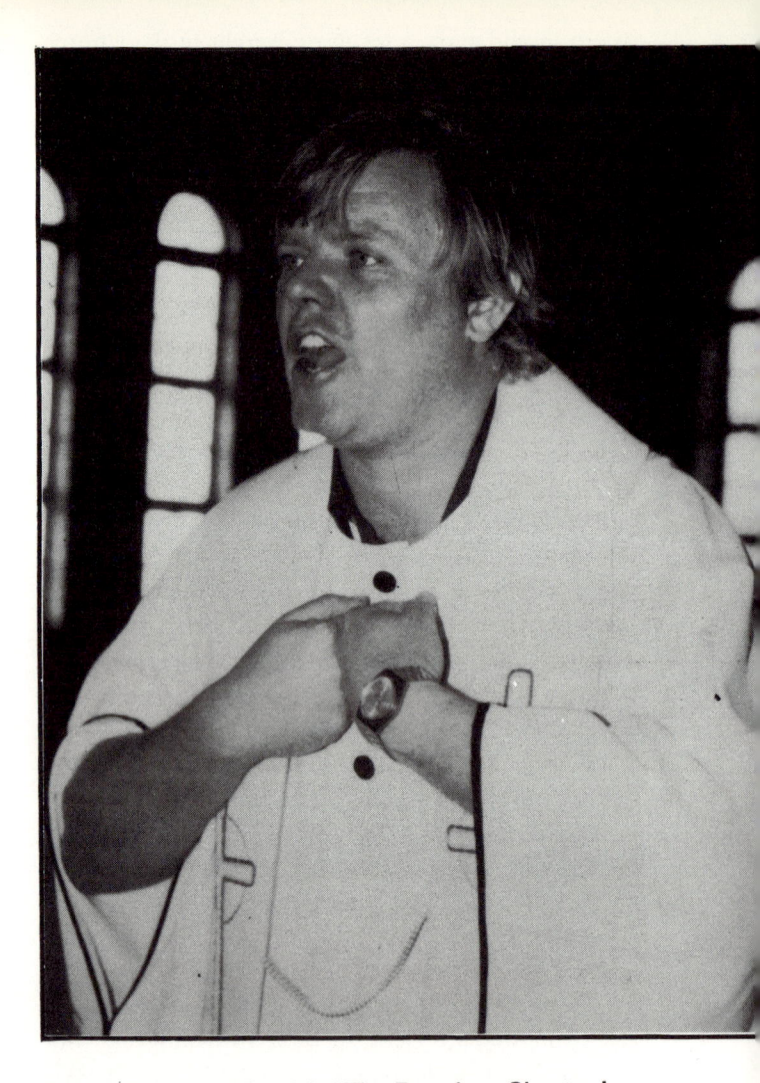

Father Chris Langeveld: "The Freedom Charter is offering us a way of making our faith effective in our lives."

minister in a very separate and unequal way to the needs of their members. Again the Freedom Charter makes sense of all that when it says "There shall be houses, security and comfort". There should be things like creches and orphanages; there should be places where the disabled and the sick will be cared for. So that's where the Church needs to involve itself.

Secondly, the Church produces a great deal of literature. A lot more could be around the issue of popularising the voice of the people contained in the Freedom Charter. To what extent is Christian literature in this country projecting the voice of the people? I think the Freedom Charter challenges the Churches to publicise the underside of history — the side of history that the state likes to wipe out.

For me, the voice of the people — the cries of the people — are a really privileged source for us Christians and for the people as a whole in South Africa. It is a way of finding out what God's will is all about. So, that's another avenue that the Church can look at.

Then there's its resources. The Church possesses numerous resources in the form of skilled, trained personnel, in the form of money, in the form of property. To what extent are these being put at the service of the oppressed people fighting for liberation and the transformation of our country?

Just to give you an example, to what extent are our Churches and our conference centres given over to people's organisations, to our people so that they can build up their organisations and their leadership? So often our structures and properties are put at the disposal of the privileged who really don't need them as much as the disenfranchised and dispossessed people of our country.

Q: Is there any message you want to give Christians about the Freedom Charter?

Langeveld: Yes, I'd like to say one thing and that's that I think up to now the Churches have evaluated apartheid, they've condemned it, they've seen it as being counter to the values of the gospels and the values of the Kingdom of God. But unfortunately many of these moral judgements and statements end up being very general and are not actually rooted sufficiently in the concrete context of the South African situation.

I'm not saying that these moral statements are not necessary. What I am saying is that they need to be contextualised. We all know that Christians are called to love, to be peacemakers and to live absolutely by the Kingdom and not by the values of the world, but what does that mean in the context of racial oppression in South Africa?

That's the nub of the question. And I think one of the few ways to concretise what it means to love and to live Kingdom values is to actually look at what the people say about their situation. The Freedom Charter, as far as I know, is the most democratic and broadly based document of the people expressing exactly what those conditions are.

In short what I'm saying is that unless our morality, our commitment and energies are contextualised, they are never going to be effective. The Freedom Charter is offering us a way of making our faith effective in our lives.

51. Solomon: Islam and the Freedom Charter

Imam H Solomon is a member of the Muslim Judicial Council and editor of "Call of Islam". He is also a former member of the UDF Western Cape executive. He says the principles of the Freedom Charter are compatible with Islamic teaching.

The Freedom Charter provides acceptable general principles for a future vision of South African society which are both basic and general enough to be acceptable to all groups in the liberatory struggle.

From the Islamic point of view, these general principles are in conformity with the Quranic verse: "Verily We have honoured the children of Adam" [Q xvii:70]. From this, Islam derives the principle that there is no distinction in dignity and fundamental rights between one man and another irrespective of race, sex or creed.

This principle is further substantiated by virtue of a prescription of Prophet Mohammed: "There is no advantage of an Arab over a non-Arab or for a white man over a black man, excepting by piety."

Like the Freedom Charter, Islam calls all people to a better acquaintance and co-operation for the good of all people in order to establish peace, based on justice for all people.

The fundamental general principles of the Freedom Charter are concerned on the whole with those fundamental rights upon which, according to Islamic belief, it is forbidden to infringe in any way. They also deal with economic, social and cultural rights where Islam does not make any distinction on the basis of race, language or religion.

Serious concern is given to the realisation of these basic rights. Islam commands that we struggle for its attainment:

"Oh you who believe! Stand out firmly for justice as witnesses to God." [Q iv:135]

An Imam speaking at the launch of the UDF in August 1983.

In the face of state repression, the people assert their own alternative. Mourners proclaim the Freedom Charter at the mass funeral of the victims of the Uitenhage massacre in March 1985.

XXIV. Organising with the Freedom Charter

52. The Freedom Charter as an organising tool

In the last few years a major task for democratic South Africans has been the building of popular mass-based organisations in all sectors of our society. How can the Freedom Charter help us in this task? This article offers some pointers.

In using the Freedom Charter in organisational work it is useful to distinguish between two levels: Firstly, educational and training work among activists and members of our organisations; and secondly, mass organisational work.

Ongoing work at the second level depends on the development of activists and members at the first level. Let us consider each of these two levels at some length.

Education and training

Most of the re-emerging mass-based organisations in our country are extremely young. It is true that they are building upon older traditions of struggle, and, in some cases, upon the experience of older people. But the great majority of our activists and organisations are youthful and relatively inexperienced.

This relative inexperience is manifested in many ways. For instance in different regions of South Africa organisations have developed to various degrees and out of different conditions. There is still a great deal of unevenness in development on a regional level. This is sometimes reflected in different styles of work and even in misunderstandings between regions.

The broad democratic movement in South Africa has also pulled together activists and members from many different class and ideological backgrounds. Within the ranks of UDF affiliates, for instance, there are activists who have emerged from the black consciousness movement, from the ultra-left Unity Movement or from white liberal circles. Some have been politicised in the trade union movement, others through involvement in housing, anti forced removals, etc. Others are veterans from the 1950s. Still others have come into the struggle in the last few months.

All of this reflects tremendous growth in a period where a new, mass-based unity is being forged. But it would be naive to imagine that this growth would not also involve many unevennesses. Without doubt, one of the main problems is the different levels of ideological development of activists and members of organisations. This unevenness sometimes makes the satisfactory resolution, or even understanding of political differences impossible. In such a situation there is always a danger that factionalism, personality differences and gossip will replace healthy political debate.

The 30th anniversary of the Freedom Charter provides an important opportunity to work towards the resolution of this particular set of problems which hamper our organisational work.

The Freedom Charter enjoys widespread support and prestige. It is therefore an important factor for unifying our ranks. More than this, the Freedom Charter emerged from the struggle of the 1950s, the last period when the development of mass organisation was possible in our country. The Freedom Charter and the process of its development and popularisation contain many organising lessons for the present.

In developing education around the demands of the Freedom Charter we are developing the level of political understanding within our ranks. Such work may result in debates and even disagreements, but the disagreements should be political and disciplined in character and not personal, factional or regional.

In carrying forward this kind of work there are a number of likely misconceptions that can hamper us.

Not a 'sacred text': There is sometimes a tendency to treat the Freedom Charter as if it were a 'sacred text', to be accepted on blind faith. Real respect for the Freedom Charter is something very different from this blind allegiance. If we are going to support the Freedom Charter we should read it carefully, discuss it, argue about it. We must take criticisms of the Freedom Charter seriously. We must understand how to defend it, if need be. Not everyone who does not accept the Freedom Charter is an enemy.

If the Freedom Charter is relevant to today's struggles, and we believe that it is, then it should not have to be protected behind a glass case in a museum.

Not a programme of action: There are other attitudes which, in supporting the Freedom Charter, try to make the Freedom Charter the answer to everything. This actually deprives it of its usefulness. You do not use a spoon to cut meat.

It is important to understand the differences between the Freedom Charter and a programme of action. A programme of action is a plan of action. It sets down tasks for particular groups of people. A programme of action also often makes deadlines, the times by which these tasks must be completed. It sets out methods of work. Programmes are essential organising tools: we need to spell out the different steps and stages involved in our various tasks. We also need programmes of action to assess how our work is going. Are we falling behind? Are we on time? The preparations for, and the organising of the Congress of the People, for instance, involved many programmes of action. But the document that emerged from the 1955 Congress of the People is *not* a programme of action. That is not a weakness of the Freedom Charter. The Charter has its own purposes and uses.

The Freedom Charter is also not itself a detailed programme of strategy and tactics. The Charter was not drawn up by any specific organisation. It was not even drawn up by the Congress Alliance, although this alliance made the Congress of the People and the Freedom Charter possible. The Charter was made by tens of thousands of South Africans, from all parts of the country. It emerged from the people's struggles and aspirations.

A detailed programme of strategy and tactics will spell out not just the broad aims of an organisation, it will deal with the *methods* for attaining these goals, and it may distinguish between different levels of work.

Such a programme may deal with the different aspects of a struggle — national and international — and the different approaches they may require. It may address the question of methods — violent or non-violent, legal or underground. The Freedom Charter is not this sort of document. Although, clearly, it can, and has, guided documents of this kind.

Not a 'democratic mask': We have seen that some supporters of the Freedom Charter treat it as if it were the answer to everything. There are other 'supporters' of the Charter who hold an equally incorrect attitude. There are some who are lukewarm, even cynical in their support of the Freedom Charter.

Such elements present the Freedom Charter as a pretty face, some attractive demands, behind which we can hide our more serious intentions.

It is possible that many of us may feel that a liberated South Africa will lead to the deepening and enriching of some of the demands in the Freedom Charter. The Charter is, for instance, not a socialist document. But this does not mean that we should be cynical, or insincere about the Freedom Charter. The spirit of the Charter is completely in harmony with the wider goals of a socialist South Africa.

In fact, socialism will deepen and guarantee the democracy and national independence that the Freedom Charter calls for. The Freedom Charter's democratic demands are not to be thrown out of the window once we advance to socialism.

Mass organisational work

So far we have dealt with the first level of work in celebrating the 30th anniversary of the Freedom Charter. We have considered how activists and **members of organisations can advance their ideological understanding of the struggle. This may provide the basis for overcoming some of our organisational problems.**

The second and most important level of work relates to mass organisational activity. In considering this level of work the anniversary in itself should not determine our programme and our priorities. We should begin with the actual conditions on the ground and ask ourselves how the anniversary of the Charter can be used to develop the struggle.

The current period is one in which the political and economic crisis of the apartheid state is deepening. The political structures in the black communities, particularly the town and community councils, are crumbling. In reply the apartheid

"Mobilising the maximum numbers" ... youth display enthusiasm for the Charter at the Jabulani Amphitheatre in Soweto in February, 1985 after hearing Nelson Mandela reject a conditional offer of release from prison.

government has applied an effective state of emergency in several regions of the country. The army and police have been sent into many townships like a foreign army of occupation.

This is also a period of economic crisis, the worst since the 1930s. The burden of sales tax, rents, transport, and unemployment is weighing heavier and heavier on our communities. This is a sickness of apartheid capitalism, but ordinary people are made to suffer the most.

In this situation we need to mobilise the maximum number of people, and we need to build mass-based organisations. We need to have a structured presence street-by-street, house-by-house. We also need to build the maximum unity between all progressive organisations, within the ranks of the United Democratic Front, and beyond.

The Freedom Charter must be built into our mass campaigns. But how? Just by handing out copies at bus queues and outside railway stations? The answer to this is clearly: "No!" The first rule of organisation is to begin where people are at in their understanding.

This means using the specific demands of the Charter and relating them to people's immediate problems — houses, the need for jobs, and so on. In this work the Charter is very useful because it speaks about particular problems, but it also joins different issues together. In mass organising we must take the people from what they know to what they do not yet understand properly.

We must mobilise people around such Charter demands as work and security, houses, security and comfort, rejection of local authorities and so on. We must then ask why there are not jobs at all, why people are not properly housed in South Africa, why the so-called representatives of the people are neither interested nor able to act on their behalf.

These issues then lead us to the wider questions, and to the two crucial demands of the Freedom Charter — the demand that *the people shall govern*, and the demand that the national wealth shall be shared. We must be able to relate these two key demands to all *other* demands and, at the same time, relate these two demands to each other.

It should be clear why the demand that the people shall govern is related to each and every basic right demanded in the Charter. So long as a racial minority monopolises the command posts of government — the administration, parliament, police, army, jails and courts — none of the other basic human rights can be meaningfully implemented. So long as the majority of South Africa's people do not have the fundamental right to vote for and stand as candidates for all bodies that make the law, they are living like foreigners in their own country without the basic right to self-determination.

In making the connection between the first demand of the Charter and all the other demands, one of our interviewees put the matter very clearly: "All the demands of the Charter point straight to parliament." MaNyembe sings this song of the 1950s:

Chief Luthuli, Dr Naiker (three times)

Yibona 'bonsimel' epalamende
These will represent us in parliament

Dr Dadoo umhol' wethu (three times)
Dr Dadoo is our leader

uyena ozosihol' epalamende
will lead us in parliament

Dr Dadoo umhol' wethu (three times)
Dr Dadoo our leader

uyena ozosihol' sisepalamende.
He's the one to lead us in parliament.

However, the question of a people's government is not the only one. As we well know, the riches of our country are not shared. Those who reap the profits are not those who labour in the factories, in the mines, on the farms. What gets produced, and whether there are jobs or not depends on profits from the bosses and not on the needs of the people.

We must ask ourselves what *sort* of people's government is needed if the wealth of our country is to be shared in a socially useful way. In conducting mass education we should raise the question of what sort of people's government will be able to ensure that "the mineral wealth beneath the soil, the banks and monopoly industry shall be transferred to the ownership of the people as a whole"?

We believe that only a people's government in which the working class plays a leading role will be able to ensure such an outcome. In our country the workers are the most numerous and disciplined class. It is the workers who occupy the crucial place in the production of our country's wealth. Only their leadership and fullest participation can ensure the meaningful sharing of our country's wealth.

The first and central demand of the Freedom Charter, that the people shall govern, can only be fully understood in relation to the question of wealth. In this way we can link these two demands together. In turn, these demands can be linked to all others, one by one, showing how they are interrelated. This is mass educational work. But it is not just a question of talking! Mass education can only be done in and through *organisation* and *campaigning* in struggle.

Our style of organisational work: If the demand that the people shall govern is central to all other demands, it must surely tell us about HOW in the present we should be organising. If one day the people are to govern, ordinary working-class people must be developing skills, knowledge, confidence. Leadership in our organisations must be drawn from the working masses.

Such leadership must also be drawn increasingly from the ranks of the African majority of our country. This will reflect the African character of our country, and correct the effects of cultural deprivation that hits that sector of our people the hardest.

The question of African leadership is linked to working-class leadership, because more Africans are workers than any other class and most working-class leadership people in South Africa are African. While encouraging African leadership does not in itself encourage working-class leadership, the two are linked. The African people are the most oppressed section of our population, irrespective of class position. Obviously, peasants, semi-peasants, workers and unemployed are more oppressed than

Dorothy Nyembe on her release from 18 years in jail. She remains committed to ensuring that "the people shall govern".

petit-bourgeois elements. But all are forced to carry passes and subjected to more serious disabilities than any other groups in South Africa, and are also culturally oppressed.

So in the leadership of our struggle, just as working-class people do not automatically rise to leadership positions, similarly African people do not automatically rise because cultural oppression has meant differences in skills and resources of all kinds. It is our duty, in this context, to encourage and develop African and working-class leadership.

To ensure all of this, our style of work must be democratic. All members of our organisations must know that the organisations are THEIRS, that they are jointly responsible for the organisations.

Democracy is not just the right to vote for parliament once every four years. Full democracy means that the majority of the people have an ongoing say in all aspects of their lives — in the communities where they live, in the places where they work, in the factories, mines or on the land, in the schools where they learn. In all these places working-class people, the great majority in our country, need to have a dominant, ongoing and meaningful say.

Mass campaigning: Finally, we must realise that the demand that the people shall govern cannot be fully realised just by building up strong democratic organisations alongside the existing apartheid state. The organisational tasks we confront require active work. We cannot sit around waiting for the course of history to inevitably unfold. If we are to realise the full potential of the Freedom Charter, it must become an integral part of our daily struggles.

XXV. Footnotes

53. Footnotes

Chapter 18

1. Albert Luthuli, *Let My People Go*, p.142.

Chapter 22

1. Albert Luthuli, *Let My People Go. An Autobiography* (Collins, Glasgow, 1963), p.144.
2. *Drum*, December, 1955.
3. Ibid.
4. Ibid.
5. Ibid. p.142.

Chapter 23

1. Z.K. Matthews, *Freedom for My People* (David Philip, Cape Town, 1983) p.194.

Chapter 26

1. Quoted by Gail M. Gerhardt, *Black Power in South Africa, The Evolution of an Ideology* (University of California Press, Berkeley, Los Angeles, 1978) p.147.
2. *City Press, 20.05.1984* quoting Jackie Hlapalosa, Azasm national organiser.

Chapter 27

1. Interview with Billy Nair, 1984.

2. For example, *No Sizwe, One Azania, One Nation* (Zed Press, London, 1979).
3. Regarding the illegality and/or criminality of apartheid see for example the *Yearbook of the International Law Commission*, 1976, vol. 2 part 2, Report of the Commission to the General Assembly on the work of its 28th Session, Chapter 3 of Draft Articles on State Responsibility, Article 19(3)(c), p.95, where it declares that an international crime may result from, *inter alia* "a serious breach on a widespread scale of an international obligation of essential importance for safeguarding the human being, such as those prohibiting slavery, genocide and *apartheid*". See also p.108.

Chapter 29

1. Some people have argued that demands purely or primarily beneficial to workers have been 'left out' or 'watered down' in the Charter. It would only have been a working-class document, they argue, if it had explicitly mentioned the workers' committees referred to when the clause on the people's wealth was motivated at the Congress of the People.

From the research that we have done it does not appear that the establishment of workers' committees to control individual production units (mentioned in the motivation) was a specific demand from people.

Certainly it was not raised in any of the demands sent in to the Congress of the People headquarters, that we have seen. There seems no evidence that it was suppressed or 'left out'. If it had been raised before the Congress of the People it certainly was not a sufficiently widely voiced demand to warrant inclusion.

The clause as it stands, we would argue, corresponds to the way workers expressed their grievances and aspirations. This is not to suggest that the way that the clause was motivated is incompatible with the terms of the Freedom Charter. It is nevertheless *an* interpretation, which, like others, will have to be struggled over.

While the Charter does not cater purely for workers, it remains, as we argue, primarily in the interests of workers.

There are also objections to the notion of a multi-class alliance, from which the Freedom Charter arose, since some argue that working class interests tend to be subordinated to those of other classes in such alliances. Crucial as such questions are, we do not discuss them here. Our concern is with the Charter as a vision of a future South Africa, not with strategy and tactics.

Chapter 42

1. A man's obligation to pay cattle or other items to the father of his intended wife, with a view to their marriage.

Chapter 48

1. Andrew Boraine, an ex-Nusas president, was a member of the Western Cape UDF executive at the time.

The new generation carries forward the democratic tradition. Nomhle Mxenge, the daughter of Griffiths and Victoria Mxenge, both leading democrats, assassinated by apartheid death squads.

XXVI. The Freedom Charter

52. The Freedom Charter
as adopted at the Congress of the People on 26 June 1955

Preamble
We, the people of South Africa, declare for all our country and the world to know:

That South Africa belongs to all who live in it, black and white, and that no government can justly claim authority unless it is based on the will of the people;

That our people have been robbed of their birthright to land, liberty and peace by a form of government founded on injustice and inequality;

That our country will never be prosperous or free until all our people live in brotherhood, enjoying equal rights and opportunities;

That only a democratic state, based on the will of the people, can secure to all their birthright without distinction of colour, race, sex or belief;

And therefore, we the people of South Africa, black and white, together equals, countrymen and brothers adopt this FREEDOM CHARTER. And we pledge ourselves to strive together, sparing nothing of our strength and courage, until the democratic changes here set out have been won.

The People Shall Govern!
Every man and woman shall have the right to vote for and stand as a candidate for all bodies which make laws;

All the people shall be entitled to take part in the administration of the country;

The rights of the people shall be the same regardless of race, colour or sex;

All bodies of minority rule, advisory boards, councils and authorities shall be replaced by democratic organs of self-government.

All National Groups Shall Have Equal Rights!

There shall be equal status in the bodies of state, in the courts and in the schools for all national groups and races;

All national groups shall be protected by law against insults to their race and national pride;

All people shall have equal rights to use their own language and to develop their own folk culture and customs;

The preaching and practice of national, race or colour discrimination and contempt shall be a punishable crime;

All apartheid laws and practices shall be set aside.

The People Shall Share In The Country's Wealth!

The national wealth of our country, the heritage of all South Africans, shall be restored to the people;

The mineral wealth beneath the soil, the banks and monopoly industry shall be transferred to the ownership of the people as a whole;

All other industries and trades shall be controlled to assist the well-being of the people;

All people shall have equal rights to trade where they choose, to manufacture and to enter all trades, crafts and professions.

The Land Shall Be Shared Among Those Who Work It!

Restriction of land ownership on a racial basis shall be ended, and all the land re-divided amongst those who work it, to banish famine and

land hunger;
The state shall help the peasants with implements, seed, tractors and dams to save the soil and assist the tillers;
Freedom of movement shall be guaranteed to all who work on the land;
All shall have the right to occupy land wherever they choose;
People shall not be robbed of their cattle, and forced labour and farm prisons shall be abolished.

All Shall Be Equal Before The Law!
No one shall be imprisoned, deported or restricted without fair trial;
No one shall be condemned by the order of any Government official;
The courts shall be representative of all the people;
Imprisonment shall be only for serious crimes against the people, and shall aim at re-education, not vengeance;
The police force and army shall be open to all on an equal basis and shall be the helpers and protectors of the people;
All laws which discriminate on the grounds of race, colour or belief shall be repealed.

All Shall Enjoy Human Rights!
The law shall guarantee to all their right to speak, to organise, to meet together, to publish, to preach, to worship and to educate their children;
The privacy of the house from police raids shall be protected by law;
All shall be free to travel without restriction from countryside to town, from province to province, and from South Africa abroad;
Pass laws, permits and all other laws restricting these freedoms shall be abolished.

There Shall Be Work And Security!

All who work shall be free to form trade unions, to elect their officers and to make wage agreements with their employers;

The state shall recognise the right and duty of all to work, and to draw full unemployment benefits;

Men and women of all races shall receive equal pay for equal work;

There shall be a forty-hour working week, a national minimum wage, paid annual leave, and sick leave for all workers, and maternity leave on full pay for all working mothers;

Miners, domestic workers, farm workers and civil servants shall have the same rights as all others who work;

Child labour, compound labour, the tot system and contract labour shall be abolished.

The Doors Of Learning And Culture Shall Be Opened!

The government shall discover, develop and encourage national talent for the enhancement of our cultural life;

All the cultural treasures of mankind shall be open to all, by free exchange of books, ideas and contact with other lands;

The aim of education shall be to teach the youth to love their people and their culture, to honour human brotherhood, liberty and peace;

Education shall be free, compulsory, universal and equal for all children;

Higher education and technical training shall be opened to all by means of state allowances and scholarships awarded on the basis of merit;

Adult illiteracy shall be ended by a mass state education plan;

Teachers shall have all the rights of other citizens;

The colour bar in cultural life, in sport and in education shall be abolished.

There Shall Be Houses, Security and Comfort!

All people shall have the right to live where they choose, to be decently housed, and to bring up their families in comfort and security;
Unused housing space to be made available to the people;
Rent and prices shall be lowered, food plentiful and no one shall go hungry;
A preventive health scheme shall be run by the state;
Free medical care and hospitalisation shall be provided for all, with special care for mothers and young children;
Slums shall be demolished and new suburbs built where all shall have transport, roads, lighting, playing fields, creches and social centres;
The aged, the orphans, the disabled and the sick shall be cared for by the state;
Rest, leisure and recreation shall be the right of all;
Fenced locations and ghettos shall be abolished and laws which break up families shall be repealed.

There Shall Be Peace And Friendship!
South Africa shall be a fully independent state, which respects the rights and sovereignty of all nations;
South Africa shall strive to maintain world peace and the settlement of all international disputes by negotiation not war;
Peace and friendship amongst all our people shall be secured by upholding the equal rights, opportunities and status of all;
The people of the protectorates Basutoland, Bechuanaland and Swaziland shall be free to decide for themselves their own future;
The right of all the peoples of Africa to independence and self-government shall be recognised, and shall be the basis of close cooperation.
Let all who love their people and their country now say, as we say here: "These freedoms we will fight for, side by side, throughout our lives, until we have won our liberty."